quick and easy
desserts

Styling SUSIE SMITH, ANNA PHILLIPS
Photography ASHLEY MACKEVICIUS

TRIDENT
PRESS
INTERNATIONAL

Introduction

*Indulge yourself with chocolate, cool off with homemade ice cream,
finish the perfect meal with the perfect dessert. Whether it's a family dinner,
a special birthday, a festive occasion, a dessert for supper or just because you
need a treat, this is the book for you. It is packed with sumptuous desserts
to suit any meal.*

*Look for the step-by-step recipes which show how easy it is to make
spectacular-looking desserts and check out the hints and tips for variations,
do ahead information, storage and variations.*

Published by:
TRIDENT PRESS INTERNATIONAL
801 12th Avenue South
Suite 400
Naples, FL 34102 U.S.A.
(c)Trident Press
Tel: (239) 649 7077
Fax: (239) 649 5832
Email: tridentpress@worldnet.att.net
Website: www.trident-international.com

Quick & Easy Desserts

Production Director: Anna Maguire
Home Economist: Donna Hay
Recipe Development: Lucy Andrews, Sheryle Eastwood
Food Photography: Ashley Mackevicius
Food Styling: Susie Smith, Anna Phillips.

Includes Index
ISBN 1582794731

Printed in Colombia

ABOUT THIS BOOK

INGREDIENTS

Unless otherwise stated the following
ingredients are used in this book:

Cream	Double, suitable for whipping
Flour	White flour, plain or standard
Sugar	White sugar

CANNED FOODS

Can sizes vary between countries and
manufacturers. You may find the quantities in this book are slightly different to
what is available. Purchase and use the
can size nearest to the suggested size in
the recipe.

MICROWAVE IT

Where microwave instructions occur in
this book, a microwave oven with an output power of 850 watts (IEC705 – 1988)
or 750 watts (AS2895 – 1986) was used.
The output power of most domestic
microwaves ranges between 600 and 900
watts (IEC705 – 1988) or 500 and 800
watts (AS2895 – 1986), so it may be necessary to vary cooking times slightly
depending on the output power of your
microwave.

WHAT'S IN A TABLESPOON?

AUSTRALIA
1 tablespoon = 20 mL or 4 teaspoons
NEW ZEALAND
1 tablespoon = 15 mL or 3 teaspoons
UNITED KINGDOM
1 tablespoon = 15 mL or 3 teaspoons
The recipes in this book were tested in
Australia where a 20 mL tablespoon is
standard. The tablespoon in the New
Zealand and the United Kingdom sets of
measuring spoons is 15 mL. For recipes
using baking powder, gelatine, bicarbonate
of soda, small quantities of flour and cornflour, simply add another teaspoon
for each tablespoon specified.

Contents

6 *Cool Desserts* 18 *Pies & Pastries* 28 *Quick & Easy*

36 *Festive* 42 *Fabulous Favourites* 52 *Light & Low Delights*

76 *Sweet Finishes*

79 *Decorative Touches*

58 *Something Spectacular* 66 *Hot Puddings* 81 *Index*

Cool Desserts

Cool, refreshing desserts make the perfect finish on a summer's day. When you want a traditional dessert with a difference, try the Orange and Lime Cheesecake. Or for a more exotic occasion, try the Mango Soup with Sorbet — it's the ideal way to complete an Oriental meal.

ORANGE AND LIME CHEESECAKE

Oven temperature
180°C, 350°F, Gas 4

155 g/5 oz plain sweet biscuits, crushed
90 g/3 oz butter, melted
desiccated coconut, toasted

ORANGE AND LIME FILLING
185 g/6 oz cream cheese, softened
2 tablespoons brown sugar
1¹/₂ teaspoons finely grated orange rind
1¹/₂ teaspoons finely grated lime rind
3 teaspoons orange juice
3 teaspoons lime juice
1 egg, lightly beaten
¹/₂ cup/125 mL/4 fl oz sweetened condensed milk
2 tablespoons cream (double), whipped

1   Place biscuits and butter in a bowl and mix to combine. Press biscuit mixture over base and up sides of a well-greased 23 cm/9 in flan tin with a removable base. Bake for 5-8 minutes, then cool.

2   To make filling, place cream cheese, sugar, orange and lime rinds and orange and lime juices in a bowl and beat until creamy. Beat in egg, then mix in condensed milk and fold in cream.

3   Spoon filling into prepared biscuit case and bake for 25-30 minutes or until just firm. Turn oven off and cool cheesecake in oven with door ajar. Chill before serving. Serve cheesecake decorated with toasted coconut.

Serves 8

When limes are unavailable lemon rind and juice can be used instead of the lime rind and juice to make an equally delicious dessert.

Orange and Lime Cheesecake

NECTARINE TIMBALES

½ cup/125 g/4 oz sugar
½ cup/90 mL/3 fl oz water
⅓ cup/90 mL/3 fl oz orange juice
6 nectarines, halved and stoned
8 teaspoons gelatine
1 cup/250 mL/8 fl oz cream (double), whipped
1 tablespoon orange-flavoured liqueur

ORANGE SAUCE
1 tablespoon sugar
rind ½ orange, cut into strips
1 cup/250 mL/8 fl oz orange juice
2 tablespoons orange-flavoured liqueur
2 teaspoons arrowroot blended with 4 teaspoons water

1 Combine sugar, water and orange juice in a saucepan. Add nectarines, bring just to the boil, then reduce heat and simmer for 4-5 minutes or until nectarines are soft. Using a slotted spoon remove nectarines and set aside. Sprinkle gelatine over hot liquid in pan and stir to dissolve.

2 Place nectarines (including skin) and cooking syrup in a food processor or blender and process until smooth. Push mixture through a sieve into a bowl, then fold in cream and liqueur. Spoon mixture into six lightly oiled timbale moulds, cover and chill until set.

3 To make sauce, place sugar, orange rind and juice, liqueur and arrowroot mixture in a saucepan and cook over a medium heat, stirring, until mixture boils and thickens. Cool. To serve, unmould timbales and accompany with sauce.

Serves 6

These melt-in-the-mouth desserts are just as delectable made with fresh peaches. If using peaches, peel before puréeing.
If you do not have timbale moulds use small, attractively shaped ramekins or teacups. If using ramekins, choose ones that have a 1 cup/ 250 mL/8 fl oz capacity.

LAYERED-FRUIT TERRINE

1 star fruit (carambola), sliced
1 peach, peeled, stoned and sliced

MANGO LAYER
2 tablespoons caster sugar
1 cup/250 mL/8 fl oz mango purée
2 tablespoons orange-flavoured liqueur
4 teaspoons gelatine dissolved in
⅓ cup/90 mL/3 fl oz hot water, cooled
¾ cup/185 mL/6 fl oz cream (double), whipped

PASSION FRUIT LAYER
2 tablespoons caster sugar
½ cup/125 mL/4 fl oz passion fruit pulp
2 tablespoons orange juice
2 tablespoons melon-flavoured liqueur
4 teaspoons gelatine dissolved in
⅓ cup/90 mL/3 fl oz hot water, cooled
¾ cup/185 mL/6 fl oz cream (double), whipped

1 Arrange star fruit (carambola) over base and up sides of a lightly oiled glass 11 x 21 cm/4½ x 8½ in loaf dish.

2 To make Mango Layer, combine sugar, mango purée and liqueur in a bowl. Stir in gelatine mixture, then fold in cream. Pour carefully into loaf dish and chill until firm.

3 To make Passion Fruit Layer, combine sugar, passion fruit pulp, orange juice and liqueur in a bowl. Stir in gelatine mixture, then fold in cream. Place a layer of peach slices over Mango Layer, then carefully pour over passion fruit mixture and chill until set. To serve, unmould terrine and cut into slices.

Serves 10

For easy removal, run a spatula around the edge of the terrine to free it from the sides of the dish, before turning out.

PINK AND WHITE ICE CREAM

1¼ cups/315 g/10 oz sugar
½ cup/125 mL/4 fl oz water
6 egg yolks
250 g/8 oz white chocolate, melted
1 teaspoon vanilla essence
2 cups/500 mL/16 fl oz cream
(double), whipped
500 g/1 lb raspberries, roughly
chopped

1 Place sugar and water in a saucepan and cook over a low heat, stirring constantly, until sugar dissolves. Bring to the boil, then reduce heat and simmer for 5 minutes or until syrup reduces by half.

2 Place egg yolks in a bowl and beat until thick and creamy. Continue beating, while adding syrup in a thin stream. Add chocolate and vanilla essence and beat until mixture thickens and is cool.

3 Fold cream and raspberries into chocolate mixture, then pour into a freezerproof container, cover and freeze until firm.

Serves 8

Serve scoops of this pretty ice cream with fresh raspberries or other fresh fruit of your choice.

DOUBLE ZABAGLIONE SOUFFLE

½ cup/100 g/3½ oz caster sugar
6 egg yolks
1 cup/250 mL/8 fl oz cream (double),
whipped
4 teaspoons gelatine dissolved in
¼ cup/60 mL/2 fl oz hot water, cooled
60 g/2 oz dark chocolate, grated
1½ tablespoons coffee-flavoured liqueur
1 teaspoon instant coffee powder
dissolved in 1 teaspoon hot water, cooled

1 Place sugar and egg yolks in a heatproof bowl over a saucepan of simmering water and cook, beating, for 5-10 minutes or until mixture is thick and fluffy. Place bowl in a pan of ice and beat until mixture is cool.

2 Fold cream and gelatine mixture into egg yolk mixture. Divide mixture into two equal portions and fold chocolate and liqueur into one portion and coffee mixture into the other.

3 Place alternate spoonfuls of each mixture into individual soufflé dishes with 3 cm/1¼ in high aluminium foil collars attached. Swirl by dragging a skewer through the mixture, then chill until set.

Serves 4

Oven temperature
200°C, 400°F, Gas 6

Soufflés are delicious served with crisp dessert biscuits such as tuiles.

HAZELNUT PINWHEELS

3/4 cup/170 g/5 1/2 oz caster sugar
5 eggs, separated
125 g/4 oz hazelnuts, toasted and
finely chopped
1/4 cup/30 g/1 oz self-raising flour,
sifted
extra caster sugar

CHOCOLATE HAZELNUT FILLING
155 g/5 oz chocolate hazelnut spread
1/2 cup/125 mL/4 fl oz cream
(double), whipped

1   Place sugar and egg yolks in a bowl and beat until thick and creamy. Fold in hazelnuts and flour.

2   Place egg whites in a separate bowl and beat until soft peaks form. Fold egg white mixture into hazelnut mixture. Pour mixture into a greased and lined 26 x 32 cm/10 1/2 x 12 3/4 in Swiss roll tin and bake for 20-25 minutes or until cake is cooked. Place a clean damp teatowel over tin and set aside to cool.

3   Turn cold cake onto a piece of greaseproof paper sprinkled with extra caster sugar. Spread with hazelnut spread and cream, then roll up from short end. Chill until required.

Serves 10

Oven temperature
180°C, 350°F, Gas 4

Serve roll cut into slices, with extra whipped cream and decorate with hazelnuts. This roll is also delicious filled with just the chocolate hazelnut spread. This variation freezes well and will slice evenly if cut while still frozen. Allow to thaw in serving dishes for 20 minutes.

TRIPLE-CHOCOLATE TERRINE

Oven temperature
180°C, 350°F, Gas 4

BUTTER CAKE
125 g/4 oz butter
1 teaspoon vanilla essence
$^1/_2$ cup/100 g/3$^1/_2$ oz caster sugar
2 eggs
1 cup/125 g/4 oz self-raising flour,
sifted
$^1/_3$ cup/90 mL/3 fl oz milk

CHOCOLATE FUDGE FILLING
125 g/4 oz butter
2 tablespoons icing sugar
90 g/3 oz dark chocolate, melted
and cooled
1 cup/250 mL/8 fl oz cream
(double), chilled

MILK CHOCOLATE MOUSSE
200 g/6$^1/_2$ oz milk chocolate, chopped
125 g/4 oz unsalted butter
2 tablespoons caster sugar
2 eggs
1 cup/250 mL/8 fl oz cream (double)
1 tablespoon dark rum
6 teaspoons gelatine dissolved in
2 tablespoons hot water, cooled

WHITE CHOCOLATE GLAZE
250 g/8 oz white chocolate
100 g/3$^1/_2$ oz unsalted butter

1 To make cake, place butter and vanilla essence in a bowl and beat until light and fluffy. Gradually beat in sugar and continue beating until mixture is creamy. Beat in eggs one at a time. Fold flour and milk, alternately, into butter mixture. Spoon mixture into a greased and lined 11 x 21 cm/4$^1/_2$ x 8$^1/_2$ in loaf tin and bake for 20-25 minutes or until cooked when tested with a skewer. Stand in tin for 5 minutes, then turn onto a wire rack to cool.

2 To make fudge filling, place butter and icing sugar in a bowl and beat until creamy. Fold in dark chocolate and cream. Chill until required.

3 To make mousse, place milk chocolate and butter in a saucepan and cook over a low heat, stirring constantly, until well blended. Cool. Place sugar and eggs in a bowl and beat until thick and creamy. Fold in chocolate mixture, cream, rum and gelatine mixture.

4 To assemble terrine, cut cake horizontally into three layers. Spread 2 layers with fudge filling and place one of these layers, filling side up, in the base of an 11 x 21 cm/4$^1/_2$ x 8$^1/_2$ in loaf tin lined with plastic food wrap. Top with half the mousse and chill for 10 minutes or until almost set. Place the second layer of filling-topped cake over the mousse with filling facing upwards. Top with remaining mousse and chill until almost set. Place remaining cake layer on top and chill until set.

5 To make glaze, place white chocolate and butter in a saucepan and cook over a low heat, stirring constantly, until well blended. Cool slightly. Turn terrine onto a wire rack, trim edges, pour over glaze to cover. Allow to set.

Serves 10

Chocolate should be stored in a dry, airy place at a temperature of about 16°C/60°F. If stored in unsuitable conditions, the cocoa butter in chocolate may rise to the surface, leaving a white film. A similar discoloration occurs when water condenses on the surface. This often happens to refrigerated chocolates that are too loosely wrapped. Chocolate affected in this way is still suitable for melting, however it is unsuitable for grating.

MANGO SOUP WITH SORBET

LIME SORBET
$^1/_2$ cup/125 g/4 oz sugar
$^1/_2$ cup/125 mL/4 fl oz water
$^1/_2$ cup/125 mL/4 fl oz white wine
2 teaspoons finely grated lime rind
$^1/_2$ cup/125 mL/4 fl oz lime juice
1 egg white

MANGO COCONUT SOUP
1.5 kg/3 lb mangoes, flesh chopped
$^1/_3$ cup/90 mL/3 fl oz orange juice
$^3/_4$ cup/185 mL/6 fl oz water
$^1/_4$ cup/60 mL/ 2 fl oz green ginger wine
2 cups/500 mL/16 fl oz coconut
milk, chilled

If fresh mangoes are unavailable drained, canned mangoes can be used instead. For this recipe you will require two 440 g/ 14 oz cans.

1 To make sorbet, place sugar, water and wine in a saucepan and cook over a low heat, stirring, until sugar dissolves. Bring to the boil, then reduce heat and simmer for 5 minutes. Cool.

2 Add lime rind and juice to sugar syrup and spoon into a freezerproof container, cover and freeze until firm. Remove sorbet from freezer, place in a bowl and beat until smooth. Place egg white in a separate bowl and beat until stiff peaks form, then fold into lime mixture. Return mixture to freezerproof container, cover and freeze until solid.

3 To make soup, purée mangoes. Add orange juice, water and ginger wine and mix to combine. Chill well. To serve, stir coconut milk into soup. Pour soup into serving bowls and top with scoops of sorbet.

Serves 6

MOUSSE-BASED ICE CREAM

6 egg yolks
$^3/_4$ cup/185 g/6 oz sugar
1 cup/250 mL/8 fl oz water
3 cups/750 mL/1$^1/_4$ pt cream (double),
whipped
2 teaspoons vanilla essence

For a true vanilla flavour, use vanilla sugar to make the sugar syrup. To make vanilla sugar, fill a large airtight container with sugar, add one or two vanilla beans (pods) and leave for several days. As you use the sugar top up with fresh sugar to keep a ready supply of vanilla sugar on hand. It is great to use for any baked products or custards where a vanilla flavour is required.

*Mango Soup with Sorbet,
White Chocolate Mousse*

1 Place egg yolks in a bowl and beat until fluffy. Place sugar and water in a saucepan and cook over a low heat, stirring constantly, until sugar dissolves. Bring to the boil and cook until syrup reaches thread stage (107°C/225°F on a sugar thermometer). Beating constantly, gradually pour syrup in a thin stream, into egg yolks and continue beating until mixture leaves a trail and is cool.

2 Fold in cream and vanilla essence. Pour into a freezerproof container and freeze until ice crystals start to form around the edges. Beat mixture until even in texture, then return to freezer. Repeat beating and freezing processes two more times, then freeze until solid.

Coffee Ice Cream: Dissolve 2 tablespoons instant coffee powder in 2 tablespoons hot water. Cool. Use in place of vanilla essence.

Raspberry Ice Cream: Fold 2 cups/ 500 mL/16 fl oz raspberry purée into mousse base with cream.

Makes 1 litre/1$^3/_4$ pt

WHITE CHOCOLATE MOUSSE

CHOCOLATE MOUSSE
185 g/6 oz white chocolate
30 g/1 oz butter
$^1/_3$ cup/75 g/2$^1/_2$ oz caster sugar
4 egg yolks
2 teaspoons brandy
1$^1/_2$ cups/375 mL/12 fl oz cream
(double), whipped

PEACH COULIS
440 g/14 oz canned peaches in natural
juice, drained
1 tablespoon caster sugar
1 tablespoon orange-flavoured
liqueur (optional)

1   To make mousse, place chocolate and butter in a saucepan and cook over a low heat, stirring, until melted and well blended. Cool.

2   Place sugar, egg yolks and brandy in a heatproof bowl over a saucepan of simmering water and cook, beating, until mixture is thick and fluffy. Remove bowl from heat and continue beating until mixture is cool. Stir in chocolate mixture, then fold in cream. Spoon into serving glasses and chill until firm.

3   To make coulis, place peaches, sugar and liqueur, if using, in a food processor or blender and process until smooth. Push coulis through a sieve.

Serves 8

To serve, spoon coulis over mousse in glasses or serve separately.
This mousse is also delicious served with an apricot or raspberry coulis.

WATERMELON SORBET

$^2/_3$ cup/170 g/5$^1/_2$ oz sugar
1$^1/_4$ cups/310 mL/10 fl oz water
2$^1/_2$ cups/625 mL/1 pt watermelon
purée
2 egg whites

The addition of alcohol to the sorbet mixture prevents it from freezing rock-hard. Sorbets that do not contain alcohol should be softened in the refrigerator for 20-30 minutes before serving to make scooping easier. To prevent the sorbet from melting too quickly, chill the serving dishes.

1 Place sugar and water in a saucepan and cook over a low heat, stirring, until sugar dissolves. Bring to the boil, then reduce heat and simmer for 10 minutes. Cool.

2 Stir watermelon purée into sugar syrup, then pour into a freezerproof container and freeze until almost solid.

3 Place sorbet in a food processor or blender and process until smooth. Place egg whites in a bowl and beat until soft peaks form, then fold into fruit mixture. Return to freezerproof container and freeze until solid.

Mango and Passion Fruit Sorbet: Replace watermelon purée with 2 cups/500 mL/16 fl oz of mango purée and the pulp of 4 passion fruit.

Kiwifruit Sorbet: Replace watermelon purée with 2 cups/500 mL/16 fl oz kiwifruit purée, $^1/_4$ cup/60 mL/2 fl oz freshly squeezed grapefruit juice and 2 tablespoons mint-flavoured liqueur.

Makes 1.2 litres/2 pt

CUSTARD-BASED ICE CREAM

1$^1/_4$ cups/280 g/9 oz caster sugar
8 egg yolks
4 cups/1 litre/1$^3/_4$ pt milk
2 cups/500 mL/16 fl oz cream (single)
2 teaspoons vanilla essence

If you don't have an ice-cream maker pour mixture into a freezerproof container and freeze until ice crystals start to form around the edges. Stir with a fork to break up ice crystals. Repeat process 2-3 times, then allow ice cream to freeze solid. The stirring ensures the finished ice cream has a smooth texture with no large ice crystals.

1 Place sugar and egg yolks in a bowl and beat until thick and creamy.

2 Place milk and cream in a saucepan and bring just to the boil. Remove from heat and whisk gradually into egg yolk mixture. Return mixture to saucepan and cook over a low heat, stirring constantly, until mixture coats the back of a wooden spoon. Place pan in a bowl of ice and cool to room temperature.

3 Stir in vanilla essence, then transfer mixture to an ice-cream maker and freeze according to manufacturer's instructions.

Chocolate Ice Cream: Reduce caster sugar to $^3/_4$ cup/170 g/5$^1/_2$ oz and fold 315 g/10 oz cooled, melted dark or milk chocolate into cooled custard.

Peach Ice Cream: Purée 2 x 440 g/ 14 oz drained, canned peaches and fold into cooled custard.

Makes 1.5 litres/2$^1/_2$ pt

SUMMER WINE JELLY

4 apricots, stoned and halved
200 g/6½ oz green seedless grapes
250 g/8 oz strawberries, halved
250 g/8 oz fresh or canned cherries,
stoned
60 g/2 oz gelatine dissolved in ½ cup/
125 mL/4 fl oz hot water, cooled
2 cups/500 mL/16 fl oz sweet
white wine
2 cups/500 mL/16 fl oz apple juice
⅓ cup/90 mL/3 fl oz melon-flavoured
liqueur or additional apple juice

1 Place apricots, grapes, strawberries
and cherries in a bowl and toss to
combine.

2 Place gelatine mixture, wine, apple
juice and liqueur or additional apple
juice in a bowl and mix to combine.
Pour one-quarter of the wine mixture
into a lightly oiled 4 cup/1 litre/1¾ pt
capacity mould, add one-quarter of the
fruit and chill until set.

3 Repeat three times to use remaining
liquid and fruit. When jelly is set
unmould and serve with extra fruit,
if desired.

Unmoulding a gelatine dessert:
Moulded gelatine desserts need to be
loosened before turning out. This is
easily done by placing the mould in
warm water for a few seconds.

After removing mould from water dry
the base and tip it sideways, while at
the same time gently pulling the set
jelly away from the edge of the mould.
This breaks the air lock. Rinse the
serving plate with cold water and place
upside down on top of the mould.
Then, holding firmly, quickly turn over
both mould and plate and give a sharp
shake. The dessert should fall onto the
plate. If it refuses to move, place a hot,
wet cloth over the base of the mould
for 10-20 seconds. Wetting the plate
means that you can easily move the
dessert if it does not land in the centre
when you unmould it.

Serves 8

Almost any fresh fruit can
be used to make this
dessert, however, avoid fresh
pineapple, pawpaw and
kiwifruit as they contain an
enzyme which prevents the
jelly from setting.

Summer Wine Jelly

Pies & Pastries

Whether it's a picnic in the park, a family dinner or a special occasion, you are sure to find the perfect pie to match the occasion in this chapter.

SOUR CREAM APPLE PIE

Oven temperature
200°C, 400°F, Gas 6

Bake blind refers to the technique which is used to bake pastry cases before filling. To bake blind, line the uncooked pastry case with nonstick baking paper then fill with baking weights, uncooked rice or dried beans. Bake as directed in the recipe, then remove weights and paper and bake a little longer as directed in recipe.

Sour Cream Apple Pie

2 quantities Sweet Shortcrust Pastry (page 21)
2 tablespoons apricot jam

APPLE FILLING
75 g/2¹/₂ oz butter
3 green apples, cored, peeled and sliced
2 tablespoons brown sugar

CARAMEL SAUCE
¹/₄ cup/60 g/2 oz sugar
4 teaspoons water
¹/₄ cup/60 mL/2 fl oz cream (double)
30 g/1 oz butter, cut into small pieces

SOUR CREAM TOPPING
2 cups/500 g/1 lb sour cream
4 teaspoons caster sugar
1 teaspoon vanilla essence

1 Roll pastry out to 5 mm/¹/₄ in thick and use to line a greased, deep 18 cm/7 in fluted flan tin with a removable base. Bake blind for 10 minutes. Remove weights and paper and bake for 8-10 minutes longer or until pastry is golden. Place jam in a saucepan and bring to the boil. Brush hot cooked pastry case with boiling jam and cook for 3-4 minutes longer. Cool.

2 To make filling, melt half the butter in a frying pan over a medium heat, add half the apples, sprinkle with half the sugar and cook, turning slices until they are tender. Remove and repeat with remaining butter, apples and sugar. Layer apples evenly in pastry case.

3 To make sauce, place sugar and water in a heavy-based saucepan and cook over a low heat, stirring until sugar dissolves. Bring to the boil and boil, without stirring, for 8 minutes or until mixture is a caramel colour. Reduce heat, carefully stir in cream and stir until sauce is smooth. Mix in butter and cool slightly. Drizzle caramel over apples in pastry case.

4 To make topping, combine sour cream, sugar and vanilla essence in a bowl. Spoon topping evenly over apples, taking mixture just to rim of pie. Reduce oven temperature to 180°C/350°F/Gas 4 and bake for 5-7 minutes. Cool at room temperature, then chill for several hours or overnight before serving.

Serves 8

RASPBERRY MOUSSE FLAN

500 g/1 lb mixed berries of
your choice
ALMOND PASTRY
1¼ cups/155 g/5 oz flour
2 tablespoons caster sugar
15 g/½ oz ground almonds
125 g/4 oz butter, cut into pieces
1 egg yolk, lightly beaten
2-3 tablespoons water, chilled

RASPBERRY MOUSSE FILLING
90 g/3 oz raspberries
¼ cup/60 g/2 oz caster sugar
2 eggs, separated
½ cup/125 mL/4 fl oz cream
(double), whipped
8 teaspoons gelatine dissolved in
½ cup/125 mL/4 fl oz hot water,
cooled

1   To make pastry, place flour, sugar and almonds in a food processor and process to combine. Add butter and process until mixture resembles fine breadcrumbs. With machine running add egg yolk and enough water to form a soft dough. Turn pastry onto a lightly floured surface and knead briefly until smooth. Wrap in plastic food wrap and chill for 30 minutes.

2   Roll out pastry on a lightly floured surface and use to line a lightly greased, deep 20 cm/8 in fluted flan tin with a removable base. Chill for 15 minutes. Line pastry case with nonstick baking paper, weigh down with baking weights, uncooked rice or dried beans and bake for 10 minutes. Remove weights and paper and bake for 10 minutes longer or until pastry case is lightly browned and cooked.

3   To make filling, purée raspberries, then push through a sieve, to remove seeds. Place sugar and egg yolks in a bowl and beat until thick and creamy. Place egg whites in a separate bowl and beat until stiff peaks form.

4   Fold cream and egg whites into egg yolk mixture. Then fold 4 tablespoons of egg mixture into raspberry purée. Fold half the gelatine mixture into the raspberry mixture and the remainder into the egg mixture.

5   Place large spoonfuls of egg mixture into pastry case, then top with smaller spoonfuls of raspberry mixture. Repeat until both mixtures are used. Run a spatula through the mousse to swirl the mixtures. Chill for 2 hours or until mousse is firm. Just prior to serving, top flan with mixed berries.

Serves 8

Raspberry Mousse Flan

When making pastry have all the utensils and ingredients as cold as possible. In hot weather, chill the utensils before using, wash your hands in cold water and use only your fingertips for kneading. Always preheat the oven before baking pastry. If pastry is put into a cold oven the fat will run and the pastry will be tough and greasy with a poor texture.

SWEET SHORTCRUST PASTRY

1½ cups/185 g/6 oz flour
125 g/4 oz butter, cut into cubes
⅓ cup/75 g/2½ oz caster sugar
¼ cup/30 g/1 oz cornflour
1 egg, lightly beaten
1 egg yolk, lightly beaten
1 teaspoon vanilla essence

1   Place flour, butter, sugar and cornflour in a food processor and process until mixture resembles coarse breadcrumbs. Combine egg, egg yolk and vanilla essence and, with machine running, slowly add to flour mixture. Continue processing until a soft dough forms.

2   Turn dough onto a lightly floured surface and knead lightly. Wrap in plastic food wrap and chill for 30 minutes. Use as desired.

Homemade shortcrust pastry is easy to make if you have a food processor. This recipe is suitable to use whenever sweet shortcrust pastry is called for.

SUGAR-CRUSTED BASKETS

Oven temperature
200°C, 400°F, Gas 6

SUGAR-CRUSTED BASKETS
6 sheets filo pastry
60 g/2 oz butter, melted
$^1/_2$ cup/125 g/4 oz sugar

POACHED FRUIT
1 cup/250 g/8 oz sugar
1 cup/250 mL/8 fl oz water
$^1/_2$ cup/125 mL/4 fl oz white wine
4 apricots, stoned and quartered
4 peaches, stoned and cut into eighths
4 plums, stoned and quartered
4 nectarines, stoned and cut into eighths
16 strawberries

RASPBERRY CREAM
125 g/4 oz raspberries, puréed
1 tablespoon icing sugar
$^3/_4$ cup/185 mL/6 fl oz cream (double), lightly whipped

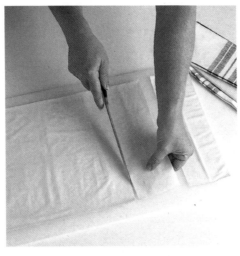

1 To make baskets, cut each pastry sheet crosswise into 8 cm/3^1/4 in wide strips. Grease outsides of four small, round-based ramekins and place upside down on a greased baking tray. Brush pastry strips with butter and lay over ramekins, overlapping each strip, and bringing ends down to lay flat on tray. Brush again with butter and sprinkle generously with sugar. Bake for 10-15 minutes or until pastry is crisp and golden.

2 To poach fruits, place sugar, water and wine in a saucepan and cook over a low heat, stirring, until sugar dissolves. Add apricots, peaches, plums and nectarines and simmer for 3-4 minutes or until fruit is just soft. Remove pan from heat, add strawberries and stand for 5 minutes. Drain.

3 To make Raspberry Cream, push raspberry pureé through a sieve to remove seeds. Fold icing sugar and purée into cream.

4 Just prior to serving, place baskets on individual serving plates, fill with poached fruits and top with Raspberry Cream.

Serves 6

These sugar-crusted baskets filled with poached fruit are ideal for entertaining as each part can be made ahead of time. Leave the final assembly until just prior to serving or the fruit will cause the pastry baskets to go soggy and collapse.

CREAMY CARAMEL BANANA PIE

Oven temperature
190°C, 375°F, Gas 5

There is a way to ensure that a biscuit crust never sticks to the pie plate and that you will always get that perfect slice. It takes a little extra time but is worth the effort. Cut a square of aluminium foil 10 cm/4 in larger than diameter of the pie plate. Turn plate upside down and press foil firmly over it. Remove foil, turn pie plate right way up and press moulded foil firmly into plate. Fold edges of foil over rim of the plate. Next, press crumb mixture firmly into foil-lined plate and bake as directed in recipe. Cool crust to room temperature then freeze for 1 hour or overnight – the crust must be frozen solid. Using edges of foil, carefully lift crust from plate and gently peel away foil a little at a time. Then, supporting base with a spatula, carefully return crust to the pie plate.

This version of the traditional American Mud Pie is sure to be popular as a dessert or as an afternoon tea treat. To make the pie really special, top with chocolate caraques (see page 79) and pipe whipped cream around the edge.

200 g/6^1/$_2$ oz gingernut biscuits, crushed
75 g/2^1/$_2$ oz butter, melted
4 teaspoons icing sugar
^{1}/$_2$ teaspoon vanilla essence
1 cup/250 mL/8 fl oz cream (double), whipped

BANANA CARAMEL FILLING
1 cup/250 mL/8 fl oz sweetened condensed milk
3 just-ripe bananas, sliced

1   Combine crushed biscuits and butter in a bowl, then press over base and up sides of a greased 20 cm/8 in pie plate and bake for 10 minutes. Cool.

2   To make filling, pour condensed milk into a shallow 20 cm/8 in pie plate. Cover with aluminium foil, taking the foil over the rim of the pie plate to make it airtight. Place pie plate in a baking dish with enough water to come halfway up the sides of the dish. Increase oven temperature to 220°C/425°F/Gas 7 and cook for 1^1/$_4$-1^1/$_2$ hours or until condensed milk is a caramel colour. Add water to dish as required during cooking. Cool caramel completely.

3   Place bananas in biscuit crust, then pour over caramel to completely cover.

4   Fold icing sugar and vanilla essence into cream. Place cream mixture in a piping bag fitted with a large star nozzle and pipe rosettes around edge of pie. Chill for at least 4 hours. This pie is best served very cold.

Serves 8

COFFEE NUT PIE

220 g/7 oz plain chocolate biscuits, crushed
125 g/4 oz butter

COFFEE FILLING
1 litre/1^3/$_4$ pt vanilla ice cream, softened
2 teaspoons instant coffee powder dissolved in 4 teaspoons hot water, cooled

CHOC-NUT TOPPING
200 g/6^1/$_2$ oz dark chocolate
^{1}/$_2$ cup/100 g/3^1/$_2$ oz caster sugar
^{1}/$_2$ cup/125 mL/4 fl oz evaporated milk
60 g/2 oz chopped pecans or walnuts

1   Combine crushed biscuits and butter in a bowl, then press over base of a greased shallow 23 cm/9 in flan dish.

2   To make filling, place ice cream and coffee mixture in a bowl and mix to combine. Spoon over biscuit base and place in freezer.

3   To make topping, place chocolate, sugar and evaporated milk in a saucepan and cook over a low heat, stirring, until chocolate melts and mixture is smooth. Stir in pecans or walnuts and cool. Pour topping over filling and freeze until firm.

Serves 6

RHUBARB AND APPLE TART

Oven temperature
200°C, 400°F, Gas 6

1 quantity Sweet Shortcrust Pastry
(page 21)

RHUBARB AND APPLE FILLING
6 stalks rhubarb, chopped
2 tablespoons sugar
30 g/1 oz butter
3 green apples, cored, peeled
and sliced
$^1/_2$ cup/125 g/4 oz cream cheese
$^1/_3$ cup/90 g/3 oz sugar
1 egg
1 teaspoon vanilla essence

For details about blind
baking see hint on page 18.

1   Roll out pastry on a lightly floured surface and use to line a greased 23 cm/ 9 in fluted flan tin with a removable base. Blind bake for 15 minutes, then remove weights and paper and bake for 5 minutes longer. Cool completely.

2   To make filling, poach or microwave rhubarb until tender. Drain well, stir in sugar and cool. Melt butter in a frying pan over a medium heat, add apples and cook, stirring, for 3-4 minutes. Cool.

3   Place cream cheese, sugar, egg and vanilla essence in a bowl and beat until smooth. Spoon rhubarb into pastry case, then top with cream cheese mixture and arrange apple slices on the top. Reduce oven temperature to 180°C/ 350°F/Gas 4 and cook for 40-45 minutes or until filling is firm.

Serves 10

ORANGE CHOCOLATE TARTS

Oven temperature
200°C, 400°F, Gas 6

375 g/12 oz prepared shortcrust pastry
125 g/4 oz dark chocolate, melted

ORANGE FILLING
2 tablespoons sugar
3 egg yolks
$1^1/_4$ cups/315 mL/10 fl oz milk, scalded
1 tablespoon finely grated orange rind
2 tablespoons orange-flavoured
liqueur
$1^1/_2$ teaspoons gelatine dissolved in
4 teaspoons hot water, cooled
$^1/_4$ cup/60 mL/2 fl oz cream (double),
whipped

For an attractive
presentation, decorate
tarts with quartered orange
slices and fine strips of
orange rind.

1   Roll pastry out and use to line six 10 cm/4 in flan tins. Blind bake for 8 minutes, then remove weights and paper and bake for 10 minutes longer or until pastry is golden. Cool completely. Brush cooled pastry cases with melted chocolate and allow chocolate to set.

2   To make filling, beat sugar and egg yolks in a heatproof bowl over a saucepan of simmering water, until a ribbon trail forms when beater is lifted from mixture. Remove bowl from heat and gradually whisk in milk. Transfer mixture to a heavy-based saucepan and cook over a low heat, stirring, until mixture thickens and coats the back of a wooden spoon. Do not allow the mixture to boil. Place pan in a bowl of ice and stir until cool.

3   Stir in orange rind, liqueur and gelatine mixture, then fold in cream, and spoon filling into pastry cases. Chill.

Serves 6

Quick & Easy

Easy and irresistible – the desserts in this chapter are ideal for impromptu gatherings or those times when you need a sweet treat.

CHOCOLATE BROWNIE TORTE

Oven temperature
180°C, 350°F, Gas 4

185 g/6 oz dark chocolate,
roughly chopped
45 g/1¹/₂ oz butter, chopped
¹/₄ cup/60 g/2 oz caster sugar
1 egg
¹/₂ teaspoon vanilla essence
60 g/2 oz slivered almonds
¹/₄ cup/30 g/1 oz flour
6 scoops ice cream, flavour of
your choice

1 Place 125 g/4 oz chocolate and butter in a heatproof bowl over a saucepan of simmering water and heat, stirring, for 5 minutes or until chocolate melts and mixture is smooth.

2 Place sugar, egg and vanilla essence in a bowl and beat until mixture is thick and creamy. Beat in chocolate mixture, then fold in almonds, flour and remaining chocolate pieces. Spoon mixture into a lightly greased and lined 20 cm/8 in sandwich tin and bake for 15-20 minutes or until cooked when tested with a skewer. Turn onto a wire rack and cool for 5-10 minutes before serving.

3 To serve, cut warm brownie into wedges and accompany with a scoop of ice cream – coffee-flavoured ice cream is a delicious accompaniment for this dessert.

Serves 6

Chocolate melts more rapidly if broken into small pieces. The melting process should occur slowly, as chocolate scorches if overheated.
The container in which chocolate is being melted should be kept uncovered and completely dry. Covering could cause condensation and just one drop of water will ruin the chocolate.

Chocolate Brownie Torte

DATES WITH ORANGE FILLING

315 g/10 oz fresh dates
$^1/_4$ teaspoon ground cinnamon
$^1/_4$ teaspoon ground cardamom
$^1/_4$ cup/60 mL/2 fl oz cognac
or brandy
1 orange, sliced
fine strips orange rind

ORANGE FILLING
125 g/4 oz mascarpone
4 teaspoons icing sugar
2 teaspoons finely grated orange rind
4 teaspoons orange juice

Serve with halved orange slices and thin strips of orange rind.
For a scrumptious after-dinner treat accompany these dates with a cup of rich coffee and an orange-flavoured liqueur.

1 Remove seeds from dates, by cutting through centre of dates lengthways then opening out. Place cinnamon, cardamom and cognac or brandy in a glass dish and mix to combine. Add dates and toss to coat. Cover and macerate for 1 hour.

2 To make filling, place mascarpone, icing sugar, orange rind and juice in a bowl and beat until light and fluffy. Spoon mascarpone mixture into a piping bag fitted with a medium-sized star nozzle.

3 Drain dates and pat dry with absorbent kitchen paper. Pipe mascarpone mixture into the centre of each date. Chill until required.

Variation: In place of the mascarpone a mixture of cream cheese and cream can be used. Beat 60 g/2 oz softened cream cheese until smooth. Whip $^1/_4$ cup/60 mL/ 2 fl oz cream (double) until soft peaks form, then fold into cream cheese. Stir in icing sugar, orange rind and juice.

Serves 4

ROCKY ROAD ICE CREAM

1 litre/1$^3/_4$ pt vanilla ice cream, softened
2 x 60 g/2 oz chocolate-coated Turkish delight bars, chopped
10 pink marshmallows, chopped
5 white marshmallows, chopped
6 red glacé cherries, chopped
6 green glacé cherries, chopped
4 tablespoons shredded coconut, toasted
2 x 45 g/1$^1/_2$ oz chocolate-coated scorched peanut bars, chopped
wafers

For a chocolate version of this easy dessert use a rich chocolate ice cream in place of the vanilla.

1 Place ice cream in a bowl, then fold in Turkish delight bars, pink and white marshmallows, red and green cherries, coconut and peanut bars. Spoon mixture into a freezerproof container, cover and freeze until firm.

2 To serve, place scoops of ice cream into bowls and serve with wafers.

Serves 6

Pancakes with Orange Sauce (page 32), Dates with Orange Filling, Rocky Road Ice Cream

PANCAKES WITH ORANGE SAUCE

1 cup/125 g/4 oz flour
$^1/_2$ teaspoon salt
$^1/_2$ teaspoon bicarbonate of soda
$1^1/_4$ cups/250 g/8 oz natural yogurt
$^1/_3$ cup/90 mL/3 fl oz milk
1 egg, lightly beaten
extra nautral yogurt (optional)

ORANGE COINTREAU SAUCE
2 tablespoons caster sugar
1 teaspoon finely grated orange rind
$^1/_2$ cup/125 mL/4 fl oz orange juice
1 teaspoon cornflour blended with
2 teaspoons water
2 tablespoons orange-flavoured
liqueur

1 Sift flour, salt and bicarbonate of soda together into a bowl. Make a well in the centre of the flour mixture. Combine yogurt, milk and egg, pour into well in dry ingredients and mix until just combined.

2 Drop spoonfuls of mixture into a heated, lightly greased, heavy-based frying pan and cook until bubbles form on the surface, then turn pancakes and cook on second side until golden.

3 To make sauce, place sugar, orange rind and juice in a saucepan and cook over a medium heat, stirring constantly, until sugar dissolves. Stir in cornflour mixture and cook for 1-2 minutes or until sauce thickens. Stir in liqueur and heat for 1-2 minutes longer. To serve, spoon sauce over pancakes and accompany with extra natural yogurt, if desired.

Serves 4

Pancakes, one of the quickest desserts you can make, can be prepared ahead of time then reheated just prior to serving. To reheat, stack pancakes in a microwavable container, cover and heat on MEDIUM (50%) for 1-2 minutes or until pancakes are hot. Take care not to overheat or the pancakes will become tough.

STUFFED LYCHEES WITH SABAYON

48 lychees, peeled and seeded
200 g/6$^1/_2$ oz blueberries

BERRY SABAYON
$^1/_3$ cup/75 g/2$^1/_2$ oz caster sugar
4 egg yolks
100 g/3$^1/_2$ oz mixed berries, puréed
and sieved

1 Stuff each lychee with a blueberry.

2 To make sabayon, place sugar and egg yolks in a heatproof bowl over a saucepan of simmering water and cook, beating, for 5-10 minutes or until mixture is thick and fluffy. Fold in puréed berries. Place lychees in serving bowls, spoon over sabayon and decorate with remaining blueberries.

Variation: Redcurrants are a delicious alternative to the blueberries in this recipe.

Serves 6

To remove seeds from lychees, cut flesh away from top of seed and gently pull seed away from flesh.

*Stuffed Lychees with Sabayon,
Chocolate Millefeuilles*

CHOCOLATE MILLEFEUILLES

1 packet chocolate cake mix
250 g/8 oz blueberries
250 g/8 oz raspberries
2 tablespoons icing sugar

CHOCOLATE CREAM
155 g/5 oz milk chocolate, melted
and cooled
2 tablespoons brandy
1 cup/250 mL/8 fl oz cream (double),
whipped

1 Prepare chocolate cake following packet directions. Divide batter between two greased and lined 26 x 32 cm/10^1/2 x 12^3/4 in Swiss roll tins and bake for 8-10 minutes or until cooked when tested with a skewer. Turn cakes onto a wire rack and cool. Using a 7.5 cm/3 in round cutter cut out twelve rounds of cake.

2 To make Chocolate Cream, fold chocolate and brandy into cream.

3 To assemble millefeuilles, spread each cake round with Chocolate Cream. Top six rounds with blueberries and six with raspberries, then sprinkle with icing sugar. Place a blueberry-topped round on a serving plate, then top with a raspberry-topped round. Just prior to serving, sprinkle with remaining icing sugar.

Serves 6

Oven temperature as per packet directions

Just raspberries or any berries of your choice can be used in place of the blueberries for these tasty dessert treats.

GINGER PEAR CAKES

Oven temperature
180°C, 350°F, Gas 4

Raw sugar is a golden to dark brown colour and is characterised by it larger crystal size and richer flavour. The amount of molasses that a sugar retains will determine its colour. Specific types of raw sugar include demerara and muscovado.

$^1/_2$ cup/125 g/4 oz raw sugar
$^1/_4$ cup/60 mL/2 fl oz vegetable oil
1 egg, lightly beaten
1 teaspoon vanilla essence
1 cup/125 g/4 oz flour
1 teaspoon bicarbonate of soda
$^1/_2$ teaspoon ground ginger
$^1/_2$ teaspoon ground nutmeg
2 pears, cored, peeled and finely diced
155 g/5 oz glacé ginger or stem ginger in syrup, chopped

GINGER CREAM
1 cup/250 mL/8 fl oz cream (double)
$^1/_4$ cup/60 g/2 oz sour cream
1 tablespoon honey
1 tablespoon brandy
$^1/_4$ teaspoon ground ginger
1 tablespoon finely chopped glacé ginger or stem ginger in syrup

1 Place sugar, oil, egg and vanilla essence in a bowl and beat to combine. Sift together flour, bicarbonate of soda, ginger and nutmeg. Mix flour mixture into egg mixture, then fold in pears and chopped ginger.

2 Spoon batter into six lightly greased large muffin tins and bake for 20 minutes. Reduce oven temperature to 160°C/325°F/Gas 3 and bake for 15-20 minutes longer, or until cakes are cooked when tested with a skewer.

3 To make Ginger Cream, place cream, sour cream and honey in a bowl and beat until soft peaks form. Add brandy and ground ginger and beat to combine. Fold in chopped ginger. Serve cakes hot or warm accompanied by Ginger Cream.

Serves 6

CREAMY FRUIT PARFAITS

Oven temperature
180°C, 350°F, Gas 4

Any fruits of your choice can be used to make this attractive dessert. Puréed, drained mangoes, peaches or apricots are all good alternatives to the fresh mango purée.

$^1/_4$ cup/60 g/2 oz sugar
$^1/_3$ cup/90 mL/3 fl oz white wine
1 tablespoon lime juice
$1^1/_4$ cups/310 mL/10 fl oz cream (double)
$^1/_3$ cup/90 mL/3 fl oz mango purée
1 mango, peeled and thinly sliced
2 kiwifruit, peeled and chopped
250 g/8 oz strawberries, sliced

1 Place sugar, wine and lime juice in a saucepan and cook over a medium heat, stirring constantly, until sugar dissolves. Cool at room temperature, then chill.

2 Place cream, mango purée and wine mixture in a bowl and beat until soft peaks form.

3 Arrange a layer of mango slices in the base of four dessert glasses and top with a spoonful of mango cream. Continue layering using kiwifruit, strawberries and mango cream, finishing with a layer of mango cream. Chill.

Serves 6

Festive

Christmas, Easter and Thanksgiving are special times for many people not only because of the religious significance, but also because it's a time when families gather and special meals are prepared.

Cassata alla Siciliana

Oven temperature
180°C, 350°F, Gas 4

4 eggs
$^1/_2$ cup/100 g/$3^1/_2$ oz caster sugar
$^3/_4$ cup/90 g/3 oz self-raising flour, sifted
$^1/_3$ cup/90 mL/3 fl oz brandy

CASSATA FILLING
$^1/_2$ cup/125 g/4 oz sugar
2 tablespoons water
375 g/12 oz ricotta cheese
100 g/$3^1/_2$ oz dark chocolate, finely chopped
60 g/2 oz glacé cherries, quartered
60 g/2 oz mixed peel, chopped
45 g/$1^1/_2$ oz unsalted pistachio nuts, chopped
$^1/_2$ cup/125 mL/4 fl oz cream (double), whipped

CHOCOLATE COATING
315 g/10 oz dark chocolate
90 g/3 oz butter

Decorate this traditional Italian dessert with glacé fruits and serve as a special Easter, Christmas or wedding feast treat.

1 Place eggs in a bowl and beat until light and fluffy. Gradually beat in caster sugar and continue beating until mixture is creamy. Fold in flour. Pour batter into a greased and lined 26 x 32 cm/$10^1/_2$ x $12^3/_4$ in Swiss roll tin and bake for 10-12 minutes or until cooked when tested with a skewer. Turn onto a wire rack to cool.

2 To make filling, place sugar and water in a saucepan and cook over a low heat, stirring constantly, until sugar dissolves. Cool. Place ricotta cheese in a food processor or blender and process until smooth. Transfer to a bowl, add chocolate, cherries, mixed peel, nuts and cream and mix to combine.

3 Line an 11 x 21 cm/$4^1/_2$ x $8^1/_2$ in loaf dish with plastic food wrap. Cut cake into slices and sprinkle with brandy. Line base and sides of prepared dish with cake. Spoon filling into dish and top with a final layer of cake. Cover and freeze until solid.

4 To make coating, place chocolate and butter in a saucepan and cook, stirring, over a low heat until melted and mixture is well blended. Allow to cool slightly.

5 Turn frozen cassata onto a wire rack and cover with coating. Return to freezer until chocolate sets.

Serves 10

Cassata alla Siciliana

FRENCH CHRISTMAS LOG

Oven temperature
180°C, 350°F, Gas 4

5 eggs
¹/₂ cup/100 g/3¹/₂ oz caster sugar
60 g/2 oz dark chocolate, melted
and cooled
¹/₂ cup/60 g/2 oz self-raising flour
6 teaspoons cocoa powder
icing sugar

RUM FILLING
1 tablespoon icing sugar
³/₄ cup/185 mL/6 fl oz cream (double)
1 tablespoon dark rum

GANACH ICING
185 g/6 oz dark chocolate
30 g/1 oz unsalted butter
²/₃ cup/170 mL/5¹/₂ fl oz cream
(double)

CHOCOLATE MUSHROOMS
1 egg white
¹/₂ teaspoon vinegar
¹/₃ cup/75 g/2¹/₂ oz caster sugar
1 teaspoon cornflour
30 g/1 oz dark chocolate, melted
1 teaspoon cocoa powder

1   Place eggs in a bowl and beat until fluffy. Gradually beat in caster sugar and continue beating until mixture is thick and creamy. Beat in chocolate. Sift together flour and cocoa powder, then fold into egg mixture. Pour mixture into a greased and lined 26 x 32 cm/10¹/₂ x 12³/₄ in Swiss roll tin and bake for 10-12 minutes or until cake is just firm.

Turn cake onto a damp teatowel dusted with cocoa powder, remove baking paper and roll up from short end. Stand for 2-3 minutes, then unroll, cover with a second damp teatowel and cool.

2   To make filling, place icing sugar, cream and rum in a bowl and beat until soft peaks form. Chill until required.

3   To make icing, place chocolate, butter and cream in a saucepan and cook, stirring constantly, over a low heat until mixture melts and is well combined. Chill until mixture thickens and is of a spreadable consistency. Beat mixture until thick.

4   To assemble log, spread cake with filling and roll up. Cover log with icing and mark with a spatula to resemble textured bark. Decorate with mushrooms and dust with icing sugar.

5   To make mushrooms, place egg white and vinegar in a bowl and beat until soft peaks form. Gradually beat in caster sugar and continue beating until mixture is thick and glossy. Fold in cornflour. Spoon mixture into a piping bag fitted with a plain nozzle and pipe seven button shapes for the tops of the mushrooms and small nobs for the stems, onto a greased and lined baking tray. Bake at 120°C/250°F/Gas ¹/₂ for 30 minutes or until meringue is crisp and dry. Cool meringues on tray, then join tops and stems, using a little melted chocolate, to make mushrooms. Sprinkle with cocoa powder.

Serves 10

Decorate serving plate with any remaining mushrooms. Cut log into slices and serve with vanilla ice cream if desired.

*French Christmas Log,
Boiled Christmas Pudding (page 40)*

BOILED CHRISTMAS PUDDING

500 g/1 lb sultanas
250 g/8 oz raisins
125 g/4 oz glacé apricots, chopped
125 g/4 oz glacé cherries, halved
125 g/4 oz blanched almonds
60 g/2 oz mixed peel
$^3/_4$ cup/185 mL/6 fl oz brandy
250 g/8 oz butter, softened
$^1/_2$ cup/90 g/3 oz brown sugar
1 tablespoon finely grated orange rind
4 eggs
4 teaspoons fresh orange juice
1 cup/125 g/4 oz flour
1 teaspoon ground cinnamon
$^1/_2$ teaspoon ground mixed spice
$^1/_2$ teaspoon ground nutmeg
4 cups/250 g/8 oz breadcrumbs made
from stale bread

If the pudding is not to be eaten immediately it may be stored in the refrigerator, wrapped in the oven bag, then reheated by reboiling in the pudding basin for 1 hour.
Check water in saucepan regularly during cooking and add more hot water as required.

1 Combine sultanas, raisins, apricots, cherries, almonds, mixed peel and brandy in a bowl and set aside.

2 Place butter, sugar and orange rind in a bowl and beat until light and creamy. Beat in eggs, one at a time, then mix in orange juice.

3 Sift together flour, cinnamon, mixed spice and nutmeg. Fold flour mixture, fruit mixture and breadcrumbs into butter mixture.

4 Spoon pudding mixture into an 8 cup/2 litre/3$^1/_2$ pt capacity pudding basin lined with an oven bag. Seal oven bag with string, place a piece of aluminium foil over pudding and seal with pudding basin lid. Place basin in a saucepan with enough water to come halfway up the sides of the basin. Boil for 4$^1/_2$-5$^1/_2$ hours or until pudding is cooked through. Serve hot, warm or cold with whipped cream or vanilla ice cream.

Serves 10-12

SPICY PUMPKIN PIE

1 quantity Sweet Shortcrust Pastry
(page 21)

SPICY PUMPKIN FILLING
280 g/9 oz pumpkin, cooked
and puréed
2 eggs, lightly beaten
$^1/_2$ cup/125 g/4 oz sour cream
$^1/_2$ cup/125 mL/4 fl oz cream (double)
$^1/_4$ cup/60 mL/2 fl oz golden syrup
$^1/_2$ teaspoon ground nutmeg
$^1/_2$ teaspoon ground mixed spice
$^1/_2$ teaspoon ground cinnamon

Oven temperature
200°C, 400°F, Gas 6

Serve pie hot, warm or cold with whipped cream.

1 To make filling, place pumpkin, eggs, sour cream, cream, golden syrup, nutmeg, mixed spice and cinnamon in a bowl and beat until smooth.

2 Roll pastry out and use to line a greased 23 cm/9 in flan tin with a removable base. Spoon filling into pastry case. Bake for 20 minutes, then reduce heat to 160°C/325°F/Gas 3 and bake for 25-30 minutes longer or until filling is set and pastry is golden. Stand pie in tin for 5 minutes before removing.

Serves 8

Fabulous Favourites

This chapter is filled with desserts that are loved around the world. Delight your family with a pavlova – the all-time favourite in Australia and New Zealand. Try your hand at an American angel food cake or the rich, smooth, creamy toffee-topped French crème brûlée. And who can resist the ever-popular English bread and butter pudding?

THE PERFECT PAVLOVA

Oven temperature
120°C, 250°F, Gas $^1/_2$

For extra crunch sprinkle the top of the pavlova with nuts. Both Australia and New Zealand claim to have created this truly marvellous dessert. However, both agree that it is named after the famous Russian ballerina.

6 egg whites
1$^1/_2$ cups/315 g/10 oz caster sugar
6 teaspoons cornflour, sifted
1$^1/_2$ teaspoons white vinegar
1$^1/_4$ cups/315 mL/10 fl oz cream (double), whipped
selection of fresh fruits, such as orange segments, sliced bananas, sliced peaches, passion fruit pulp, berries or sliced kiwifruit

1 Place egg whites in a bowl and beat until soft peaks form. Gradually beat in sugar and continue beating until mixture is thick and glossy.

2 Fold cornflour and vinegar into egg white mixture. Grease a baking tray and line with nonstick baking paper. Mark a 23 cm/9 in diameter circle on paper, then grease and dust with flour.

3 Place one-quarter of the egg white mixture in the centre of the circle and spread out to within 3 cm/1$^1/_4$ in of the edge. Pile remaining mixture around edge of circle and neaten using a metal spatula or knife. Bake for 1$^1/_2$-2 hours or until firm to touch. Turn off oven and cool pavlova in oven with door ajar. Decorate cold pavlova with cream and top with fruit.

Serves 8

The Perfect Pavlova

BLACKBERRY CREME BRULEE

200 g/6¹/2 oz blackberries
2 cups/500 mL/16 fl oz cream (double)
1 vanilla bean (pod)
1 cup/220 g/7 oz caster sugar
5 egg yolks

TOFFEE TOPPING
¹/2 cup/125 g/4 oz sugar
¹/4 cup/60 mL/ 2 fl oz water

Any fruit or a mixture of berries can be used instead of the blackberries. If using fruits such as apricots, plums or peaches they will need to be lightly poached first.

1   Divide berries between six ¹/2 cup/ 125 mL/4 fl oz capacity ramekins. Place cream and vanilla bean (pod) in a saucepan and bring to the boil. Place caster sugar and egg yolks in a bowl and beat until thick and creamy. Continue beating while slowly pouring in hot cream. Return mixture to pan and cook over a low heat, stirring, until mixture thickens. Remove vanilla bean (pod). Pour cream mixture into ramekins and refrigerate until custards are set.

2   To make topping, place sugar and water in a saucepan and cook over a medium heat, stirring, until sugar dissolves. Bring mixture to the boil and boil, without stirring, until sugar syrup is golden. Swirl pan once or twice during cooking. Carefully spoon toffee over cold brûlées and set aside to harden.

Serves 6

BERRY CHOCOLATE MUD CAKE

Oven temperature
120°C, 250°F, Gas ¹/2

315 g/10 oz dark chocolate
250 g/8 oz butter, chopped
5 eggs, separated
2 tablespoons caster sugar
¹/4 cup/30 g/1 oz self-raising flour, sifted
250 g/8 oz raspberries
whipped cream, for serving

RASPBERRY COULIS
250 g/8 oz raspberries
sugar to taste

1   Place chocolate and butter in a heatproof bowl over a saucepan of simmering water and heat, stirring, until chocolate melts and mixture is smooth. Cool slightly.

2   Beat egg yolks and caster sugar into chocolate mixture, then fold in flour.

3   Place egg whites in a separate bowl and beat until stiff peaks form. Fold egg whites and raspberries into chocolate mixture. Pour into a greased and lined 20 cm/8 in round cake tin and bake for 1¹/4 hours or until cooked when tested with a skewer. Turn off oven and cool cake in oven with door ajar.

4   To make coulis, place raspberries in a food processor or blender and process until puréed. Push purée through a sieve to remove seeds. Add sugar to taste. Serve cake with coulis and cream.

Serves 10

Berry Chocolate Mud Cake,
Blackberry Crème Brûlée

JAFFA SELF-SAUCING PUDDING

125 g/4 oz butter
2 teaspoons finely grated orange rind
3/4 cup/170 g/5 1/2 oz caster sugar
2 eggs
100 g/3 1/2 oz chocolate chips
1 1/2 cups/185 g/6 oz self-raising
flour, sifted
1/2 cup/125 mL/4 fl oz orange juice
1/4 cup/30 g/1 oz cocoa powder
1/2 cup/100 g/3 1/2 oz caster sugar
1 1/2 cups/375 mL/12 fl oz boiling
water

1 Place butter and orange rind in a bowl and beat until light and fluffy. Gradually beat in sugar and continue beating until mixture is creamy.

2 Beat in eggs one at a time. Toss chocolate chips in flour, then fold flour mixture and orange juice, alternately, into batter. Spoon batter into a greased ovenproof dish.

3 Sift cocoa powder and sugar together over batter in dish, then carefully pour over boiling water. Bake for 40 minutes or until pudding is firm.

Serves 8

Oven temperature
180°C, 350°F, Gas 4

Serve this simple family dessert with vanilla or chocolate ice cream or lightly whipped cream.

COCONUT ANGEL FOOD CAKE

Oven temperature
180°C, 350°F, Gas 4

$^3/_4$ cup/90 g/3 oz flour
$^1/_4$ cup/30 g/1 oz cornflour
1 cup/220 g/7 oz caster sugar
10 egg whites
$^1/_2$ teaspoon salt
1 teaspoon cream of tartar
8 teaspoons water
1 teaspoon vanilla essence
45 g/1$^1/_2$ oz shredded coconut

FLUFFY FROSTING
1$^1/_4$ cups/315 g/10 oz sugar
$^1/_2$ cup/125 mL/4 fl oz water
3 egg whites
90 g/3 oz shredded coconut, lightly
toasted

1 Sift flour and cornflour together
three times, then sift once more with
$^1/_4$ cup/60 g/2 oz of the caster sugar.

2 Place egg whites, salt, cream of
tartar and water in a bowl and beat
until stiff peaks form. Beat in vanilla
essence, then fold in remaining sugar,
1 tablespoon at a time.

3 Sift flour mixture over egg white
mixture then gently fold in. Lastly
sprinkle coconut over top of batter and
fold in. Spoon batter into an ungreased
angel cake tin, then draw a spatula
gently through the mixture to break up
any large air pockets. Bake for

45 minutes. When cake is cooked
invert tin and allow the cake to hang
while it is cooling.

4 To make frosting, place sugar and
water in a saucepan and cook over a
medium heat, without boiling and
stirring constantly, until sugar dissolves.
Brush any sugar from sides of pan using
a pastry brush dipped in water. Bring
the syrup to the boil and boil rapidly
for 3-5 minutes, without stirring, or
until syrup reaches the soft-ball stage
(115°C/239°F on a sugar thermometer).
Place egg whites in a bowl and beat
until soft peaks form, then continue
beating while pouring in syrup in a thin
stream. Continue beating until all syrup
is used and frosting stands in stiff peaks.
Spread frosting over top and sides of
cold cake, then press toasted coconut
onto sides of cake.

Serves 12

An angel cake tin is a
deep-sided ring tin with a
removable base that has a
centre tube higher than the
outside edges. If you do not
have an angel cake tin use
an ordinary deep-sided ring
tin with a removable base.
However, when you invert
the tin for the cake to cool,
place the tube over a
funnel or bottle. Never
grease an angel cake tin as
this stops the cake rising.

LEMON SULTANA CHEESECAKE

Oven temperature
220°C, 425°F, Gas 7

Orange rind and juice are tasty alternatives to the lemon in this recipe.

PASTRY
$^1/_2$ cup/60 g/2 oz flour
$^1/_4$ cup/30 g/1 oz cornflour
$^1/_4$ cup/30 g/1 oz custard powder
4 teaspoons icing sugar
60 g/2 oz butter
1 egg yolk
iced water

CHEESECAKE FILLING
$^1/_2$ cup/100 g/3$^1/_2$ oz caster sugar
2 teaspoons finely grated lemon rind
375 g/12 oz cream cheese, softened
$^1/_4$ cup/45 g/1$^1/_2$ oz natural yogurt
2 eggs
1 teaspoon vanilla essence
170 g/5$^1/_2$ oz sultanas

LEMON TOPPING
$^1/_2$ cup/125 mL/4 fl oz cream (double)
2 teaspoons lemon juice
$^1/_2$ teaspoon finely grated lemon rind

1 To make pastry, sift flour, cornflour, custard powder and icing sugar together into a bowl. Using fingertips, rub in butter until mixture resembles coarse breadcrumbs. Make a well in the centre of the flour mixture, then stir in egg yolk and enough water to make a firm dough. Wrap in plastic food wrap and chill for 30 minutes.

2 Roll out pastry to fit the base of a greased 20 cm/8 in springform tin. Using a fork, prick pastry base and bake for 10 minutes. Cool.

3 To make filling, place caster sugar, lemon rind, cream cheese, yogurt, eggs and vanilla essence in a bowl and beat until smooth. Fold in sultanas. Spoon mixture into prepared cake tin. Reduce oven temperature to 180°C/350°F/Gas 4 and bake for 20-25 minutes or until filling is firm. Turn off oven and cool cheesecake in oven with door ajar.

4 To make topping, place cream, lemon juice and rind in a saucepan and bring to simmering, then simmer, stirring, for 5 minutes or until mixture thickens. Pour topping over cooled cheesecake and chill until required.

Serves 8

Left: Lemon Sultana Cheesecake
Right: Devil's Food Cake

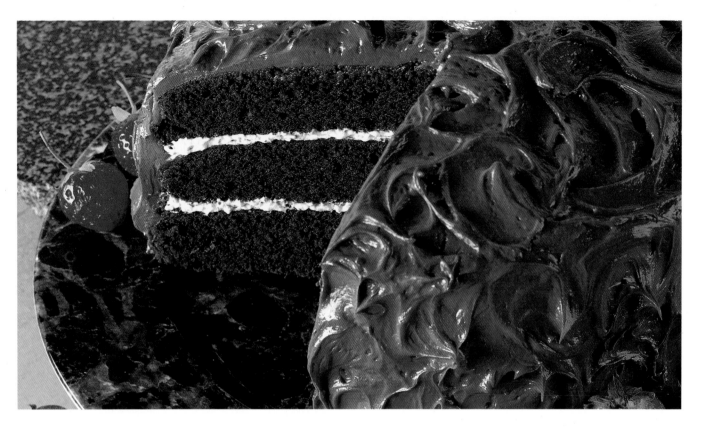

DEVIL'S FOOD CAKE

1 cup/100 g/3¹/₂ oz cocoa powder
1¹/₂ cups/375 mL/12 fl oz boiling water
375 g/12 oz unsalted butter, softened
1 teaspoon vanilla essence
1¹/₂ cups/315 g/10 oz caster sugar
4 eggs
2¹/₂ cups/315 g/10 oz flour
¹/₂ cup/60 g/2 oz cornflour
1 teaspoon bicarbonate of soda
1 teaspoon salt
¹/₂ cup/125 mL/4 fl oz cream
(double), whipped

CHOCOLATE BUTTER ICING
250 g/8 oz butter, softened
1 cup/155 g/5 oz icing sugar, sifted
2 egg yolks
1 egg
185 g/6 oz dark chocolate, melted
and cooled

1   Combine cocoa powder and water in a bowl and mix until blended. Cool. Place butter and vanilla essence in a bowl and beat until light and fluffy.

Gradually beat in caster sugar and continue beating until mixture is creamy. Beat in eggs, one at a time.

2   Sift together flour, cornflour, bicarbonate of soda and salt. Fold flour mixture and cocoa mixture, alternately, into egg mixture.

3   Divide batter between three greased and lined 23 cm/9 in sandwich tins and bake for 20-25 minutes or until cakes are cooked when tested with a skewer. Stand cakes in tins for 5 minutes before turning onto wire racks to cool.

4   To make icing, place butter in a bowl and beat until light and fluffy. Beat in icing sugar, egg yolks and egg. Beat in chocolate and continue beating until icing is thick. Sandwich cakes together using whipped cream then cover top and sides with icing.

Serves 12

Oven temperature
180°C, 350°F, Gas 4

The uniced, undecorated layers of this cake can be frozen in an airtight container for up to 3 months.

FRUITY BREAD PUDDING

Oven temperature
180°C, 350°F, Gas 4

Allowing the pudding to stand for an hour before baking allows the bread to absorb the cream mixture, resulting in the cooked pudding having a softer and moister texture.

60 g/2 oz butter
$^1/_2$ cup/90 g/3 oz brown sugar
440 g/14 oz canned sliced apples
90 g/3 oz sultanas
$^1/_2$ teaspoon ground cinnamon
12 thick slices fruit loaf, buttered and crusts removed
$1^1/_4$ cups/310 mL/10 fl oz milk
$^3/_4$ cup/185 mL/6 fl oz cream (double)
3 eggs
$^1/_2$ teaspoon vanilla essence

1   Melt butter in a frying pan over a medium heat, add sugar and cook, stirring constantly, until sugar dissolves. Stir in apples, sultanas and cinnamon and cook for 1-2 minutes longer. Cool.

2   Cut bread into triangles and arrange one-third, buttered side up, in the base of a greased ovenproof dish. Top with half the apple mixture and another layer of bread. Spoon over remaining apple mixture, then top with another layer of bread and finally arrange remaining triangles around the edges.

3   Place milk, cream, eggs and vanilla essence in a bowl and whisk to combine. Carefully pour into dish, then place dish in a baking dish with enough water to come halfway up the sides. Bake for 45-50 minutes or until pudding is firm and top is golden.

Serves 8

BANANA FRITTERS

Fruit fritters are always popular, especially with children. You might like to make these using other fruits, such as apples, peaches or canned pineapple rings.

4 large firm bananas, cut in half then split lengthways
2 tablespoons lime juice
vegetable oil for deep-frying

BATTER
1 cup/125 g/4 oz self-raising flour
2 tablespoons caster sugar
$^1/_2$ cup/125 mL/4 fl oz milk
1 egg, lightly beaten
1 egg white

CARAMEL SAUCE
$^1/_2$ cup/125 g/4 oz sugar
$^1/_2$ cup/125 mL/4 fl oz water
$^1/_2$ cup/125 mL/4 fl oz cream (double)
2 teaspoons whisky (optional)

1   To make batter, sift flour in a bowl and make a well in the centre. Combine caster sugar, milk and egg, then mix into flour mixture to make a batter of a smooth consistency. Stand for 10 minutes.

2   To make sauce, place sugar and water in a saucepan and cook over a low heat, stirring constantly, until sugar dissolves. Bring to the boil, then reduce heat and simmer, without stirring, for 5 minutes or until mixture is golden.

3   Remove pan from heat and carefully stir in cream and whisky, if using. Return pan to a low heat and cook, stirring, until combined. Cool.

4   Beat egg white until soft peaks form, then fold into batter. Heat oil in a saucepan until a cube of bread dropped in browns in 50 seconds. Brush bananas with lime juice, dip in batter to coat then drain off excess. Cook bananas in hot oil for 2-3 minutes or until golden. Serve immediately with sauce.

Serves 4

Light & Low
Delights

Low in calories and light in texture, these sinfully delicious desserts are hardly wicked at all. Even if you are not on a diet, these desserts make the perfect finish.

Coeur a la Creme

185 g/6 oz cottage cheese
60 g/2 oz reduced-fat cream cheese
1 tablespoon icing sugar
$^1/_4$ cup/60 mL/2 fl oz cream (double)
$^1/_2$ teaspoon vanilla essence
1 tablespoon orange-flavoured liqueur
250 g/8 oz mixed fruits, such as berries of your choice, plums, peaches or melons

1   Place cottage cheese in a food processor or blender and process until smooth. Add cream cheese, icing sugar, cream and vanilla essence and process to combine.

2   Line four coeur à la crème moulds with a double thickness of damp muslin or gauze and pack cheese mixture into moulds. Place moulds on a wire rack, on a tray. Cover and refrigerate for 24 hours. Turn crèmes onto serving plates, sprinkle each with a little liqueur and garnish with fruit.

Coeur à la crème moulds: These are china, heart-shaped moulds with draining holes in the base. Before lining with the muslin you should rinse them in cold water, but do not dry. You can make your own moulds, using small empty plastic containers. Cut the containers down to make sides of about 2.5 cm/1 in, then, using a skewer, punch holes in the base. These moulds will not be heart-shaped like the traditional ones but the dessert will still look and taste wonderful.

Serves 4

Start preparing this dessert the day before serving as it has to sit in the refrigerator overnight.

Coeur à la Crème

PEACH COMPOTE

6 firm ripe peaches, halved and stoned
1 cup/250 mL/8 fl oz red wine
2-3 tablespoons honey
1 cinnamon stick

Other fruits such as nectarines, plums, apples and pears are also good prepared in this way. Remember the cooking time will be a little longer for harder fruits.

Cut peaches into thick slices. Place wine, honey and cinnamon stick in a saucepan and bring to the boil, reduce heat and simmer for 5 minutes. Add peaches and cook for 5-10 minutes or until slightly softened. Cool, then chill.

Serves 4

RHUBARB FOOL

Oven temperature
190°C, 375°F, Gas 5

750 g/1¹/₂ lb rhubarb, trimmed and cut into 1 cm/¹/₂ in pieces
1 cup/170 g/5¹/₂ oz brown sugar
¹/₄ teaspoon ground cloves
2 tablespoons lemon juice
2 tablespoons orange juice
¹/₂ teaspoon vanilla essence
³/₄ cup/185 mL/6 fl oz cream (double)
¹/₂ cup/100 g/3¹/₂ oz natural yogurt

ORANGE BISCUITS
75 g unsalted butter
¹/₄ cup/60 g/2 oz caster sugar
1 egg
1¹/₂ teaspoons grated orange rind
³/₄ cup/90 g/3 oz flour

1 Place rhubarb, brown sugar, cloves, lemon and orange juices and vanilla essence in a saucepan. Bring to the boil, then reduce heat and simmer, stirring occasionally, for 15 minutes or until rhubarb is soft and mixture thick. Chill.

2 Place cream in a bowl and beat until soft peaks form. Fold yogurt into cream, then fold in chilled rhubarb mixture to give a marbled effect. Spoon into individual serving glasses and chill.

3 To make biscuits, place butter and caster sugar in a bowl and beat until light and creamy. Add egg and orange rind and beat to combine. Stir in flour. Place teaspoons of mixture, 5 cm/2 in apart, on lightly greased baking trays and bake for 10 minutes or until golden. Stand biscuits on trays for 1 minute before transferring to wire racks to cool. Accompany each fool with two or three biscuits.

Serves 8

Rhubarb is the edible stalk of the rhubarb plant and as such is in fact a vegetable. However, because of the way it is used we tend to think of it as a fruit. The leaves of the rhubarb plant are very toxic and should never to cooked or eaten.

RASPBERRY TARTS

HAZELNUT PASTRY
1 cup/125 g/4 oz flour, sifted
60 g/2 oz unsalted butter, chopped
30 g/1 oz hazelnuts, ground
1 tablespoon icing sugar
1 egg, lightly beaten
1 egg yolk, lightly beaten

CREAM FILLING
375 g/12 oz reduced-fat cream cheese
2 tablespoons caster sugar
1/4 cup/60 mL/2 fl oz cream (double)

RASPBERRY TOPPING
350 g/11 oz raspberries
1/3 cup/100 g/3 1/2 oz raspberry jam,
warmed and sieved

1 To make pastry, place flour, butter, hazelnuts and icing sugar in a food processor and process until mixture resembles fine breadcrumbs. Add egg and egg yolk, and process to form a soft dough. Wrap dough in plastic food wrap and chill for 1 hour.

2 Knead pastry lightly, then roll out to 3 mm/1/8 in thick and use to line six lightly greased 7 1/2 cm/3 in flan tins. Bake pastry cases blind for 10 minutes. Remove weights and paper and bake for 15 minutes or until golden. Cool.

3 To make filling, place cream cheese, and caster sugar in a bowl and beat until smooth. Beat cream until soft peaks form, then fold into cream cheese mixture. Cover and chill for 20 minutes.

4 To assemble, spoon filling into pastry cases, then arrange raspberries attractively on top. Brush warm jam over raspberries and chill for a few minutes to set glaze.

Serves 6

Oven temperature
200°C, 400°F, Gas 6

Any berries such as strawberries, blueberries or blackberries can be used to make these divine individual tarts. For more information about baking blind see hint on page 18.

Peach Compote, Raspberry Tarts

*Apple Pudding, Rhubarb Fool
served with Orange Biscuits
(page 54)*

APPLE PUDDING

Oven temperature
200°C, 400°F, Gas 6

The Ricotta Cream served
with this pudding is a
delicious alternative to
cream. You might like to try
it as an accompaniment to
other desserts.

6 green apples, cored, peeled and cut
into 1 cm/^{1}/$_2$ in slices
100 g/3^1/$_2$ oz raisins
60 g/2 oz pine nuts, toasted
1 cup/250 mL/8 fl oz orange juice
^{1}/$_4$ cup/90 g/3 oz honey
60 g/2 oz ground almonds
1 tablespoon finely grated orange rind
6 whole cloves
^{1}/$_2$ teaspoon ground cinnamon

RICOTTA CREAM
100 g/3^1/$_2$ oz fresh ricotta cheese
100 g/3^1/$_2$ oz cottage cheese
1-2 tablespoons milk
1-2 tablespoons caster sugar

1   Layer apples, raisins and pine nuts
in a shallow ovenproof dish. Pour over
orange juice, then drizzle with honey,
and scatter with almonds, orange
rind, cloves and cinnamon. Cover
dish with aluminium foil and bake for
35-40 minutes or until apples are tender.

2   To make cream, place ricotta and
cottage cheeses in a food processor or
blender and process until smooth. Add
a little milk if the mixture is too thick
and sweeten with sugar to taste. Serve
with apple pudding.

Serves 4

INDIVIDUAL SUMMER PUDDINGS

$^1/_2$ cup/100 g/3$^1/_2$ oz caster sugar
2 cups/500 mL/16 fl oz water
875 g/1$^3/_4$ lb mixed berries, such as
raspberries, strawberries, blueberries
or blackberries
14 slices white bread, crusts removed

BERRY SAUCE
2 tablespoons icing sugar
155 g/5 oz mixed berries, such as
raspberries, strawberries, blueberries
or blackberries
2 tablespoons water
1 tablespoon fresh lemon juice

1   Place caster sugar and water in a saucepan and cook over a low heat, stirring constantly, until sugar dissolves. Bring to the boil, then reduce heat, add berries and simmer for 4-5 minutes or until fruit is soft, but still retains its shape. Remove from heat. Drain, reserving liquid, and set aside to cool.

2   Cut 8 rounds of bread to fit the base of $^1/_2$ cup/125 mL/4 fl oz capacity ramekins. Line four ramekins with 4 rounds of the bread, reserve the remaining rounds for tops of puddings. Cut remaining bread slices into fingers and line the sides of the ramekins, trimming bread to fit if necessary. Spoon fruit into ramekins then pour over enough reserved liquid to moisten bread well. Cover with remaining bread rounds. Reserve any remaining liquid. Cover tops of ramekins with aluminium foil, top with a weight, and refrigerate overnight.

3   To make sauce, place icing sugar, berries, water and lemon juice in a food processor or blender and process to make a purée. Push mixture through a sieve to remove seeds and chill.

4   Turn puddings onto serving plates, spoon sauce over or pass separately.

Serves 4

Use either fresh or frozen berries to make this dessert. For an attractive serving presentation garnish with additional berries and accompany with natural yogurt or Ricotta Cream (see recipe on page 56).

Individual Summer Puddings

Something Spectacular

For a special occasion, a fabulous home-cooked dinner followed by a spectacular dessert is the perfect way to celebrate.

AUSTRIAN COFFEE CAKE

Oven temperature
180°C, 350°F, Gas 4

4 eggs, separated
¹/4 cup/60 g/2 oz caster sugar
45 g/1¹/2 oz ground almonds
3 teaspoons instant coffee powder
dissolved in 4 teaspoons boiling
water, cooled
¹/2 teaspoon vanilla essence
¹/4 cup/30 g/1 oz flour
chocolate-coated coffee beans or
chocolate dots
finely grated chocolate

COFFEE CREAM
1 tablespoon caster sugar
1 teaspoon instant coffee powder
dissolved in 2 teaspoons boiling
water, cooled
2 tablespoons coffee-flavoured liqueur
1 cup/250 mL/8 fl oz cream (double),
whipped

Chocolate-coated coffee beans are available from specialty food shops and some supermarkets.

1 Place egg yolks and sugar in a bowl and beat until thick and creamy. Beat in almonds, coffee mixture and vanilla essence.

2 Place egg whites in a bowl and beat until stiff peaks form. Sift flour over egg yolk mixture and fold in with egg white mixture. Spoon batter into a greased and lined 20 cm/8 in springform tin and bake for 20-25 minutes or until cooked when tested with a skewer. Stand in tin for 10 minutes, before turning onto a wire rack to cool.

3 To make Coffee Cream, mix sugar, coffee mixture and liqueur into cream. Split cold cake horizontally and use a little of the Coffee Cream to sandwich halves together. Spread remaining Coffee Cream over top and sides of cake. Decorate top of cake with coffee beans or chocolate dots and grated chocolate. Chill and serve cut into slices.

Austrian Coffee Cake

Serves 10

ORANGE AND ALMOND GATEAU

Oven temperature
180°C, 350°F, Gas 4

75 g/2¹/2 oz flaked almonds, toasted

SOUR CREAM ORANGE CAKE
1 cup/220 g/7 oz caster sugar
3 eggs
4 teaspoons orange juice
1 tablespoon finely grated orange rind
1³/4 cups/220 g/7 oz flour
¹/4 cup/30 g/1 oz cornflour
1¹/2 teaspoons baking powder
1 teaspoon bicarbonate of soda
1 cup/250 g/8 oz sour cream, lightly
beaten
250 g/8 oz butter, melted and cooled

ORANGE SYRUP
¹/2 cup/125 g/4 oz sugar
¹/4 cup/60 mL/2 fl oz orange juice
¹/4 cup/60 mL/2 fl oz orange-flavoured
liqueur

ORANGE BUTTER CREAM
¹/2 cup/125 g/4 oz sugar
¹/2 cup/125 mL/4 fl oz water
4 egg yolks
250 g/8 oz unsalted butter, softened
2 teaspoons finely grated orange rind
¹/4 cup/60 mL/2 fl oz orange juice
2 tablespoons orange-flavoured
liqueur

1 To make cake, place caster sugar, eggs, orange juice and rind in a bowl and beat until thick and creamy. Sift together flour, cornflour, baking powder and bicarbonate of soda. Place sour cream and butter in a bowl and whisk lightly to combine. Fold flour and sour cream mixtures, alternately, into egg mixture.

2 Spoon batter into three lightly greased and lined 23 cm/9 in sandwich tins and bake for 15-20 minutes or until cooked when tested with a skewer.

3 To make syrup: Five minutes before cakes complete cooking, place sugar, orange juice and liqueur in a saucepan and cook over a medium heat, stirring constantly, until sugar dissolves.

4 Turn cakes onto wire racks and, using a skewer, pierce surface of cakes to make holes that reach about halfway through the cakes. Spoon hot syrup over hot cakes and cool.

5 To make butter cream, place sugar and water in a saucepan and cook over a medium heat, stirring constantly, until sugar dissolves. Bring syrup to the boil and cook until mixture reaches the soft-ball stage (115°C/239°F on a sugar thermometer). Place egg yolks in a bowl, then beat to combine and continue beating while slowly pouring in sugar syrup. Beat for 5 minutes longer or until mixture cools and is of a thick mousse-like consistency. In a separate bowl beat butter until light and creamy, then gradually beat into egg yolk mixture. Beat in orange rind and juice and liqueur.

6 To assemble, sandwich cakes together with a little butter cream, then spread remaining butter cream over top and sides of cake. Press almonds around sides of cake.

Serves 10

The secret to this spectacular cake is to pour the hot sugar syrup over the cooked cakes while they are still hot. Do not pour cold syrup over hot cakes or hot syrup over cold cakes or the cakes will become soggy.

Orange and Almond Gâteau

FRESH BERRY TART

A combination of cream cheese and cream can be used in place of the mascarpone in this recipe if you wish. Place 250 g/8 oz softened cream cheese in a food processor and process until smooth. Add 250 mL/ 8 fl oz cream (double) and beat until mixture is creamy. The tart can also be made in a 25 cm/10 in round flan tin.

1 quantity Sweet Shortcrust Pastry
(page 21)
500 g/1 lb mixed berries

MASCARPONE ORANGE FILLING
500 g/1 lb mascarpone
2 tablespoons icing sugar
1 teaspoon finely grated orange rind
3/4 cup/185 mL/6 fl oz orange juice
1/4 cup/60 mL/2 fl oz orange-flavoured
liqueur

STRAWBERRY GLAZE
1/4 cup/75 g/2 1/2 oz strawberry jam
1/2 cup/125 mL/4 fl oz orange juice
2 teaspoons gelatine

1 Roll out pastry to fit a 23 cm/9 in square flan tin with a removable base. Bake blind for 10-15 minutes, then remove weights and paper and cook for 5-10 minutes longer or until pastry is golden. Cool.

2 To make filling, place mascarpone, icing sugar, orange rind and juice and liqueur in a bowl and beat to combine. Spoon filling into cold pastry case, then top with berries.

3 To make glaze, place jam and orange juice in a saucepan, sprinkle over gelatine and heat over a low heat until gelatine dissolves. Cool slightly, then brush over tart.

Serves 8

FILLED CHOCOLATE CUPS

This dessert is delicious garnished with crushed praline. To make praline, place 1 cup/250 g/8 oz sugar and 1 cup/250 mL/ 8 fl oz water in a saucepan and cook over a low heat, stirring, until sugar dissolves. Increase heat and simmer until syrup is golden. Scatter 3 tablespoons slivered, toasted almonds on a greased baking tray, then pour over toffee. Allow to harden then break into pieces. Place in a food processor and process until toffee resembles coarse breadcrumbs.

440 g/14 oz milk chocolate, melted

PEACH CREAM
1 1/4 cups/315 mL/10 fl oz cream
(double)
2 tablespoons icing sugar, sifted
2 peaches, peeled, stoned and
flesh puréed
1/4 cup/60 mL/2 fl oz passion
fruit pulp

PEACH COULIS
3 peaches, peeled, stoned and
flesh puréed
1/3 cup/90 mL/3 fl oz passion
fruit pulp
sugar

1 To make chocolate cups, cut six 15 cm/6 in squares of nonstick baking paper. Place small moulds or ramekins upside down on a tray and cover with paper squares. Spoon chocolate over base of mould and allow to run down sides of paper. Spread chocolate with a small spatula if it does not run freely. Allow chocolate to set, then carefully peel off paper.

2 To make Peach Cream, place cream in a bowl and beat until soft peaks form. Fold in icing sugar, peach purée and passion fruit pulp.

3 To make coulis, push peach purée and passion fruit pulp through a sieve to make a smooth purée. Add sugar to taste. To assemble, flood serving plates with coulis, place chocolate cups on plates and fill with Peach Cream.

Serves 6

RASPBERRY TRUFFLE CAKES

Oven temperature
180°C, 350°F, Gas 4

$^1/_2$ cup/45 g/1$^1/_2$ oz cocoa powder, sifted
1 cup/250 mL/8 fl oz boiling water
1$^3/_4$ cups/400 g/12$^1/_2$ oz caster sugar
125 g/4 oz butter
1$^1/_2$ tablespoons raspberry jam
2 eggs
1$^2/_3$ cups/200 g/6$^1/_2$ oz self-raising
flour, sifted
410 g/13 oz dark chocolate, melted
raspberries for garnishing

RASPBERRY CREAM
125 g/4 oz raspberries, puréed
and sieved
$^1/_2$ cup/125 mL/4 fl oz cream
(double), whipped

CHOCOLATE SAUCE
125 g/4 oz dark chocolate
$^1/_2$ cup/125 mL/4 fl oz water
$^1/_4$ cup/60 g/2 oz caster sugar
1 teaspoon brandy (optional)

3 Spoon mixture into eight lightly greased $^1/_2$ cup/125 mL/4 fl oz capacity ramekins or large muffin tins. Bake for 20-25 minutes or until cakes are cooked when tested with a skewer. Stand cakes in tins for 5 minutes then turn onto wire racks to cool. Turn cakes upside down and scoop out centre leaving a 1 cm/$^1/_2$ in shell. Spread each cake with chocolate to cover top and sides, then place right way up on a wire rack.

4 To make cream, fold raspberry purée into cream. Spoon cream into a piping bag fitted with a large nozzle. Carefully turn cakes upside down and pipe in cream to fill cavity. Place right way up on individual serving plates.

5 To make sauce, place chocolate and water in a saucepan and cook over a low heat, stirring, for 4-5 minutes or until chocolate melts. Add sugar and continue cooking, stirring constantly, until sugar dissolves. Bring just to the boil, then reduce heat and simmer, stirring, for 2 minutes. Cool for 5 minutes, then stir in brandy, if using. Cool sauce to room temperature and serve with cakes.

Serves 8

These rich little chocolate cakes filled with a raspberry cream and served with a bittersweet chocolate sauce are a perfect finale to any dinner party. Follow the step-by-step instructions and you will see just how easy this spectacular dessert is.

1 Dissolve cocoa powder in boiling water, then cool.

2 Place sugar, butter and jam in a bowl and beat until light and fluffy. Beat in eggs one at a time, adding a little flour with each egg. Fold remaining flour and cocoa mixture, alternately, into butter mixture.

Hot Puddings

You will find the puddings of childhood memories in this chapter. Pancakes, crumbles and self-saucing puddings along with soufflés and cobblers will remind you of the puddings that mother used to make. Served on their own or with custard and ice cream these desserts are a wonderful way to end a winter meal.

RHUBARB SOUFFLE

Oven temperature
220°C, 425°F, Gas 7

500 g/1 lb rhubarb, trimmed and
cut into 2.5 cm/1 in pieces
$^1/4$ cup/60 g/2 oz sugar
$^1/2$ cup/125 mL/4 fl oz water
4 teaspoons cornflour blended with
$^1/4$ cup/60 mL/2 fl oz water
$^1/2$ cup/100 g/3$^1/2$ oz caster sugar
5 egg whites
icing sugar, sifted

1 Place rhubarb, sugar and water in a saucepan and cook over a medium heat for 10 minutes or until rhubarb is soft.

2 Stir in cornflour mixture and cook for 2-3 minutes longer or until mixture thickens. Stir in half the caster sugar and cool slightly.

3 Place egg whites in a bowl and beat until soft peaks form. Gradually beat in remaining caster sugar and continue beating until mixture is thick and glossy. Fold in rhubarb mixture and spoon into a greased 20 cm/8 in soufflé dish. Bake for 15-20 minutes or until soufflé is well risen and golden. Dust with icing sugar and serve immediately.

Serves 8

Step 1 of this recipe can be cooked in the microwave. Place rhubarb, sugar and water in a microwavable dish and cook on HIGH (100%) for 5-8 minutes or until rhubarb is tender.

Rhubarb Soufflé

BRANDIED PLUM CLAFOUTI

Oven temperature
180°C, 350°F, Gas 4

500 g/1 lb plums, quartered
and stoned
$^1/_3$ cup/90 mL/3 fl oz brandy
2 tablespoons sugar
$^1/_4$ cup/30 g/1 oz flour, sifted
$^1/_4$ cup/60 g/2 oz caster sugar
1 cup/250 mL/8 fl oz milk
3 eggs, lightly beaten

BRANDY ORANGE SAUCE
2 tablespoons sugar
$^1/_2$ teaspoon ground cinnamon
$^3/_4$ cup/185 mL/6 fl oz orange juice
2 teaspoons arrowroot blended with
4 teaspoons water

1 Place plums and brandy in a bowl, sprinkle with sugar, cover and stand for 30 minutes. Drain plums and reserve liquid. Arrange plums in a lightly greased shallow ovenproof dish.

2 Place flour and caster sugar in a bowl, make a well in the centre, then stir in milk and eggs and mix to make a smooth batter. Pour batter evenly over plums and bake for 45-50 minutes or until firm.

3 To make sauce, place sugar, cinnamon, orange juice, arrowroot mixture and reserved liquid from fruit in a saucepan and cook over a medium heat, stirring constantly, until mixture boils and thickens. Serve with clafouti.

Serves 4

Clafouti is a wonderful classic French pudding, traditionally made with fresh cherries. This recipe uses plums, but you might like to try apricots, peaches, nectarines or, of course, cherries.

TOFFEE FIGS WITH SABAYON

1 cup/250 g/8 oz sugar
$^1/_2$ cup/125 mL/4 fl oz water
2 tablespoons brandy
6 fresh figs, halved

MARSALA SABAYON
$^1/_3$ cup/90 g/3 oz sugar
4 egg yolks
$^1/_4$ cup/60 mL/2 fl oz Marsala or
dry sherry

1 Place sugar and water in a saucepan and cook over a low heat, stirring constantly, until sugar dissolves. Stir in brandy, bring to the boil and cook until golden. Remove pan from heat, dip figs in toffee, then plunge into iced water for a few seconds to harden.

2 To make sabayon, place sugar and egg yolks in a heatproof bowl over a saucepan of simmering water and cook, beating, for 5-10 minutes or until mixture forms a ribbon. Beat in Marsala or sherry. To serve, spoon sabayon over figs.

Serves 4

This dessert is also delicious made using other fresh fruit such as apples, pears, apricots and strawberries.

*Brandied Plum Clafouti,
Toffee Figs with Sabayon,
Berry Pancakes with Sauce (page 74)*

APPLE AND BERRY CRUMBLE

Oven temperature
180°C, 350°F, Gas 4

¹/4 cup/60 g/2 oz caster sugar
¹/2 cup/125 mL/4 fl oz water
4 green apples, peeled, cored
and sliced
440 g/14 oz canned blueberries,
drained

CRUMBLE TOPPING
1³/4 cups/250 g/8 oz crushed
shortbread biscuits
45 g/1¹/2 oz unsalted butter, softened
4 tablespoons ground almonds
2 tablespoons demerara sugar
¹/2 teaspoon ground cinnamon
1 egg yolk
1¹/2 tablespoons cream (double)

1 Place caster sugar and water in a
saucepan and cook over a medium heat,
stirring constantly, until sugar dissolves.
Bring to the boil, then add apples and
cook, over a low heat, for 8-10 minutes
or until apples are tender. Cool.

2 Drain apples and place in a shallow
ovenproof dish. Add blueberries and
mix to combine.

3 To make topping, place crushed
biscuits, butter, almonds, demerara
sugar, cinnamon, egg yolk and cream in
a bowl and mix until just combined.
Scatter topping over fruit mixture and
bake for 20-25 minutes or until golden.

Serves 6

Blueberries have been used
to make this delicious
crumble, but blackberries,
raspberries or strawberries
are equally delicious.
Serve with natural or fruit-
flavoured yogurt.

PEACH AND BERRY COBBLER

Oven temperature
180°C, 350°F, Gas 4

2 x 440 g/14 oz canned sliced
peaches, drained
440 g/14 oz canned blackberries,
drained
4 teaspoons cornflour blended with
¹/4 cup/60 mL/2 fl oz water
1 tablespoon brown sugar

COBBLER DOUGH
¹/2 cup/60 g/2 oz self-raising flour
¹/4 cup/30 g/1 oz flour
2 tablespoons caster sugar
60 g/2 oz butter
1 egg, lightly beaten
2 teaspoons milk

1 To make dough, sift flours together
into a bowl. Stir in caster sugar, then
using fingertips, rub in butter, until
mixture resembles fine breadcrumbs.
Make a well in the centre of the dry
ingredients, then add egg and milk and
mix to form a soft dough.

2 Arrange peaches and blackberries in
a greased, shallow ovenproof dish, then
pour over cornflour mixture. Drop
heaped spoonfuls of dough around edge
of dish, then sprinkle with brown sugar
and bake for 30-35 minutes or until
topping is golden.

Serves 6

As with most fruit desserts
other fruits can be used for
this one. You might like to try
the following combinations:
apricots and apples; pears
and blueberries; or apples
and blackberries.

Apple and Berry Crumble,
Peach and Berry Cobbler

HAZELNUT CREPES

³/4 cup/90 g/3 oz flour
90 g/3 oz hazelnuts, ground
1¹/4 cups/315 mL/10 fl oz milk
1 egg, lightly beaten
2 teaspoons hazelnut or vegetable oil

ORANGE AND LIME TOPPING
1 lime
¹/2 cup/100 g/3¹/2 oz caster sugar
¹/4 cup/60 mL/2 fl oz ginger wine
2 oranges, peeled, white pith removed
and segmented

For the topping on these delicious crêpes lemon can be used in place of the lime.

1 Sift flour into a bowl, then stir in hazelnuts. Make a well in the centre of the flour mixture, then stir in milk, egg and oil. Mix to make a smooth batter, cover and stand for 30 minutes.

2 To make topping, remove rind from lime using a vegetable peeler and cut into thin strips. Set aside. Squeeze juice from lime and place in a saucepan with sugar and ginger wine. Cook over a medium heat, stirring constantly, until sugar dissolves. Bring to the boil, then reduce heat and simmer for 4 minutes. Remove pan from heat and stir in lime rind and orange segments. Cool slightly.

3 Pour 2-3 tablespoons batter into a heated, greased crêpe pan and cook over a medium heat until lightly browned on both sides. Remove from pan and repeat with remaining mixture to make eight crêpes.

4 To serve, fold crêpes into triangles, place two on each serving plate, spoon over topping and serve immediately.

Serves 4

NUTTY PLUM CRUMBLE

Oven temperature
180°C, 350°F, Gas 4

4 x 440 g/14 oz canned dark plums,
drained and ³/4 cup/185 mL/6 fl oz
liquid reserved
1 teaspoon finely grated orange rind

CRUMBLE TOPPING
¹/2 cup/60 g/2 oz flour
1 teaspoon ground mixed spice
60 g/2 oz butter, chopped
¹/3 cup/60 g/2 oz brown sugar
90 g/3 oz hazelnuts, chopped

Accompany with whipped cream or yogurt for a really wonderful family dessert.

1 To make topping, place flour and mixed spice in a bowl, then using fingertips, rub in butter until mixture resembles fine breadcrumbs. Stir in sugar and hazelnuts.

2 Place plums, reserved liquid and orange rind in a greased, shallow ovenproof dish. Toss to combine, then scatter with topping and bake for 30-35 minutes or until topping is golden.

Serves 6

*Nutty Plum Crumble,
Hazelnut Crêpes*

BERRY PANCAKES WITH SAUCE

1¹/2 cups/185 g/6 oz self-raising flour
¹/3 cup/75 g/2¹/2 oz caster sugar
2 teaspoons finely grated lemon rind
2 eggs, separated
1¹/2 cups/375 mL/12 fl oz milk
30 g/1 oz butter, melted
155 g/5 oz blueberries

BERRY SAUCE
90 g/3 oz raspberries
³/4 cup/185 mL/6 fl oz water
¹/4 cup/90 mL/3 fl oz light corn syrup
4 teaspoons arrowroot blended with
¹/3 cup/90 mL/3 fl oz water
1 tablespoon lemon juice
90 g/3 oz strawberries, quartered

1   Place flour, sugar and lemon rind in a bowl. Add egg yolks, milk and butter and mix to combine. Place egg whites in a separate bowl and beat until soft peaks form, then fold into batter with blueberries. Cook spoonfuls of mixture in a lightly greased preheated frying pan for 2-3 minutes each side or until golden. Keep warm.

2   To make sauce, place raspberries, water, corn syrup, arrowroot mixture and lemon juice in a saucepan and cook over a medium heat, stirring, for 4-5 minutes or until sauce boils and thickens. Add strawberries and mix gently to combine. To serve, spoon sauce over pancakes and serve.

Serves 4

Pancakes can be made in advance, stacked between sheets of freezer wrap and frozen in an airtight container for 2-3 months. Reheat before using. For details on reheating see hint on page 32.

APRICOT PIE

¹/2 quantity Sweet Shortcrust Pastry
(page 21)

APRICOT FILLING
3 x 440 g/14 oz canned apricot
halves, drained and sliced
¹/4 cup/45 g/1¹/2 oz brown sugar
¹/2 teaspoon ground nutmeg
¹/2 teaspoon ground cinnamon

1   To make filling, place apricots, sugar, nutmeg and cinnamon in a bowl and mix to combine.

2   Spoon filling into a greased 23 cm/ 9 in pie plate. Roll out pastry to 3 mm/ ¹/8 in thick. Mark centre of pastry and cut four 10 cm/4 in slits, crossing at the centre. Place pastry over filling and trim edges 5 mm/¹/4 in wider than rim of plate. Fold back flaps of pastry from centre of pie. Make a large scalloped edge by placing your thumb against the inside pastry edge and moulding the pastry around it with fingers of other hand.

3   Bake pie for 20-30 minutes or until pastry is golden and cooked through.

Serves 6

Oven temperature
200°C, 400°F, Gas 6

Reroll leftover scraps of pastry, then cut out decorative shapes and use to decorate tops of pies.

CHERRY PIE

1 quantity Sweet Shortcrust Pastry
(page 21)
CHERRY FILLING
3 x 440 g/14 oz canned, pitted
black cherries, drained
2 tablespoons brown sugar
4 teaspoons flour
1 teaspoon ground mixed spice

1   To make filling, place cherries on sheets of absorbent kitchen paper to absorb excess moisture. Place cherries, sugar, flour and mixed spice in a bowl and mix to combine.

2   Roll out two-thirds of the pastry to 3 mm/^{1}/8 in thick and use to line a greased 23 cm/9 in pie dish. Spoon filling into pastry case. Roll out remaining pastry and cut into 2 cm/^{3}/4 in wide strips. Twist each strip and arrange in a lattice pattern over filling. Brush edge of pie with a little water and seal each strip to edge.

3   Bake pie for 20 minutes, then reduce temperature to 160°C/325°F/ Gas 3 and bake for 30-40 minutes longer or until pastry is golden and cooked through.

Serves 6

Oven temperature
220°C, 425°F, Gas 7

Instead of making a lattice topping on this pie you might like to cut out leaf shapes and arrange them in an overlapping pattern on top of the pie. The whole top need not be covered, just make sure that the pattern is symmetrical.

APPLE PIE

1^1/2 quantities Sweet Shortcrust
Pastry (page 21)
APPLE FILLING
2 x 440 g/14 oz canned sliced apples
^{1}/4 cup/60 g/2 oz sugar
^{1}/2 teaspoon ground cloves
^{1}/2 teaspoon ground cardamom

1   To make filling, place apples, sugar, cloves and cardamom in a bowl and mix to combine.

2   Roll out two-thirds of the pastry to 3 mm/^{1}/8 in thick and use to line a greased 23 cm/9 in pie dish. Spoon filling into pastry shell.

3   Roll out remaining pastry to fit over top of pie. Cut out two apple shapes on opposite sides of pastry. Brush pastry with a little water and place apple shapes on pastry between cut-outs. Place pastry over filling, trim edge and fold under bottom pastry layer. To form a rope edging, pinch edge at a slant using your thumb and index finger and at the same time pulling back with your thumb.

4   Bake pie for 20 minutes, then reduce temperature to 160°C/325°F/ Gas 3 and bake for 30-40 minutes longer or until pastry is golden and cooked through.

Serves 6

Oven temperature
220°C, 425°F, Gas 7

Sweet Finishes

CHOCOLATE CHESTNUT TRUFFLES

100 g/3^1/$_2$ oz dark chocolate, melted

CHESTNUT FILLING
^{1}/$_4$ cup/60 mL/2 fl oz cream (double)
315 g/10 oz finely chopped
dark chocolate
30 g/1 oz butter
2 tablespoons brandy
^{1}/$_2$ cup/220 g/7 oz canned chestnut
purée

1 Spread the inside of 36 small aluminium foil cases with the melted chocolate. Allow to set.

2 To make filling, place cream in a saucepan and bring to the boil. Remove pan from the heat, add chopped chocolate and butter and whisk, using a balloon whisk, until chocolate melts and mixture is smooth. Whisk in brandy, then stir in chestnut purée.

3 Transfer mixture to a bowl, cover with plastic food wrap and chill for 2-3 hours.

4 Spoon filling into a piping bag fitted with a small fluted nozzle and pipe swirls into chocolate cases. Chill for 1 hour or until firm. Store in an airtight container in the refrigerator for up to 2 weeks.

Makes 36

Florentines (page 78), Sweet Cinnamon Bows, Chocolate Chestnut Truffles, Miniature Profiteroles (page 78)

SWEET CINNAMON BOWS

250 g/8 oz cream cheese
250 g/8 oz unsalted butter
1 cup/125 g/4 oz flour
$^{1}/_{4}$ cup/60 g/2 oz caster sugar
2 teaspoons ground cinnamon
icing sugar, sifted

1 Roughly chop cream cheese and butter and stand at room temperature for 10 minutes. Place flour, caster sugar and cinnamon in a food processor and process briefly to sift. Add cream cheese and butter and process, using the pulse button, until mixture is combined. Turn dough onto a lightly floured surface, gather into a ball and knead briefly. Wrap in plastic food wrap and chill for at least 1 hour.

2 Roll out dough to 3 mm/$^{1}/_{8}$ in thick, then cut into strips 1 cm/$^{1}/_{2}$ in wide and 20 cm/8 in long. Shape each strip into a bow and place on baking trays lined with nonstick baking paper. Cover and chill for 15 minutes. Bake for 5 minutes, then reduce temperature to 150°C/300°F/Gas 2 and bake for 10-15 minutes or until bows are puffed and golden. Cool on wire racks, then store in airtight containers. Just prior to serving sprinkle with icing sugar.

Makes 50

Oven temperature
190°C, 375°F, Gas 5

MINIATURE PROFITEROLES

Oven temperataure
250°C, 500°F, Gas 9

45 g/1¹/2 oz butter, cut into pieces
²/3 cup/170 mL/5¹/2 fl oz water
¹/2 cup/60 g/2 oz flour, sifted
2 eggs

CREME PATISSIERE FILLING
2 cups/500 mL/16 fl oz milk
¹/2 cup/100 g/3¹/2 oz caster sugar
5 egg yolks
2 tablespoons flour, sifted
4 teaspoons cornflour, sifted
2 tablespoons coffee-flavoured liqueur
2 teaspoons instant coffee powder
dissolved in 2 teaspoons boiling
water, cooled

Other liqueurs and
flavourings can be used to
flavour the filling if you wish.
For an orange filling use
2 tablespoons orange-
flavoured liqueur and
1 teaspoon finely grated
orange rind in place of the
coffee mixture and coffee-
flavoured liqueur.
For an attractive finish
decorate profiteroles with
melted chocolate as shown
in picture on previous page.

1 Place butter and water in a saucepan and bring to the boil. Using a wooden spoon, quickly stir in flour, then cook over a low heat, beating constantly, for 2 minutes or until mixture leaves sides of pan. Cool slightly. Beat in eggs, one at a time, then continue beating until mixture is glossy. Spoon batter into a piping bag fitted with a large fluted nozzle and pipe swirls onto wet baking trays lined with nonstick baking paper.

Bake for 8 minutes, then bake pastries with oven door ajar for 10 minutes or until golden and crisp. Make a slit in the base of each pastry, reduce oven temperature to 120°C/250°F/Gas ¹/2 and bake for 5 minutes or until centres dry out. Cool on wire racks.

2 To make filling, place milk in a saucepan and bring just to the boil. Cool for 10 minutes. Place sugar and egg yolks in a bowl and beat until thick and creamy. Whisk in flour and cornflour, then slowly whisk in warm milk. Pour into a clean saucepan and bring to the boil over a medium heat, beating constantly with a wooden spoon, until mixture thickens. Beat liqueur and coffee mixture into filling, then cover surface of filling with plastic food wrap. Cool.

3 Spoon cold filling into a piping bag fitted with a plain nozzle and pipe filling into profiteroles.

Makes 30

FLORENTINES

Oven temperature
180°C, 350°F, Gas 4

45 g/1¹/2 oz butter
¹/4 cup/45 g/1¹/2 oz brown sugar
2 tablespoons honey
¹/4 cup/30 g/1 oz flour sifted with
¹/4 teaspoon ground ginger
45 g/1¹/2 oz slivered almonds
30 g/1 oz glacé cherries, chopped
1 tablespoon mixed peel, chopped
100 g/3¹/2 oz dark chocolate, melted

For a professional finish to
the florentines, when the
chocolate on the base is
almost set, mark wavy lines
in it using a fork.

1 Place butter, sugar and honey in a saucepan and bring to the boil. Cool

for 5 minutes. Stir flour mixture, almonds and cherries into butter mixture. Drop teaspoons of mixture 8 cm/3¹/4 in apart onto baking trays lined with nonstick baking paper. Bake for 12-15 minutes or until brown and crisp. Stand on trays for 1 minute then transfer to wire racks to cool.

2 Spread underside of each florentine with melted chocolate.

Makes 50

Decorative
Touches

CHOCOLATE

Chocolate curls and shavings: Can be made by running a vegetable peeler down the side of a block of chocolate. If the chocolate is cold you will get shavings, if at room temperature, curls.

Chocolate caraques: Are made by spreading a layer of melted chocolate over a marble, granite or ceramic work surface. Allow the chocolate to set at room temperature. Then, holding a metal pastry scraper or large knife at a 45° angle slowly push it along the work surface away from you to form chocolate into cylinders. If chocolate shavings form, then it is too cold and it is best to start again.

Chocolate leaves: Choose non-poisonous, fresh, stiff leaves with raised veins. Retain as much stem as possible. Wash leaves, then dry well on absorbent kitchen paper. Brush the underside of leaves with melted chocolate and allow to set at room temperature. When set, carefully peel away leaf. Use one leaf to decorate an individual dessert, or make a bunch and use to decorate a larger dessert or cake.

Piped chocolate decorations: Are quick and easy to make. Trace a simple design onto a sheet of paper. Tape a sheet of baking or greaseproof paper to your work surface and slide the drawings under the paper. Place melted chocolate into a paper or material piping bag and, following the tracings, pipe thin lines. Allow to set at room temperature and then carefully remove, using a metal spatula. If you are not going to use these decorations immediately, store them in an airtight container in a cool place.

FROSTED FRUITS

Frosted, strawberries, cherries, small bunches of grapes or redcurrants make wonderful decorations for cold desserts and cakes.

To frost fruit: Rinse fruit and drain well on absorbent kitchen paper. Break into small bunches or single pieces and

FEATHERED ICING

This technique is most effective if you use Glacé Icing. To make Glacé Icing, place 200 g/6^1/$_2$ oz sifted pure icing sugar in a bowl and beat in ^{1}/$_3$-^{1}/$_2$ cup/ 90-125 mL/3-4 fl oz warm water to make an icing of spreadable consistency. Mix in ^{1}/$_4$ teaspoon vanilla essence. Glacé Icing should be used immediately. Before covering cake place 2 tablespoons of icing in a separate bowl and colour with a few drops of food colouring. Stand cake on a wire rack and pour over plain Glacé Icing. Place coloured icing in a piping bag and pipe thin straight lines across cake surface. Draw a skewer across the lines at 2 cm/^{3}/$_4$ in intervals and then back in the opposite direction between the original lines. This technique works well for all shapes of cakes.

For a spider web effect on a round cake, start at the centre and pipe the icing in a spiral. Then, starting at the centre, divide the cake into eight portions by dragging a skewer out towards the edge. Finally divide the cake eight more times by dragging the skewer in the opposite direction between the original lines.

remove any leaves or unwanted stems. Place an egg white in a small bowl and whisk lightly. Dip fruit in egg white. Remove, set aside to drain slightly, then coat with caster sugar. Stand on a wire rack to dry for 2 hours or until set. Frosted fruit is best used on the day you do it, but will keep for 12 hours in an airtight container.

You can also crystallise miniature roses, rose petals and mint leaves using this method.

QUICK DECORATING IDEAS
Flaked almonds, chopped nuts (such as pistachios, pecans and macadamias), and chopped or grated chocolate are all good for decorating the sides of cakes. Spread the sides with butter icing then roll them in your chosen decoration. Try the following decorating suggestions:
- chocolate sprinkles
- hundreds and thousands
- chocolate thins
- warmed sieved jam
- glacé and dried fruits
- sifted icing sugar
- cinnamon sugar
- sugared violets
- crushed meringue
- sifted cocoa powder
- wafer biscuit rolls
- strawberry halves dipped in chocolate

INDEX

Almond
    and Orange Gâteau 60
    Pastry 20
Angel Food Cake, Coconut 46
Apple
    and Berry Crumble 70
    and Rhubarb Tart 26
    Pie 75
    Pudding 56
    Sour Cream Pie 18
Apricot Pie 74
Austrian Coffee Cake 58

Banana
    Creamy Caramel Pie 24
    Fritters 50
Baskets, Sugar-crusted 22
Berry
    and Apple Crumble 70
    and Peach Cobbler 70
    Chocolate Mud Cake 44
    Individual Summer Puddings 57
    Pancakes with Sauce 74
    Sabayon 32
    Sauce 57, 74
    Tart, Fresh 62
Biscuits
    Florentines 78
    Orange 54
    Sweet Cinnamon Bows 77
Blackberry Crème Brûlée 44
Boiled Christmas Pudding 40
Brandied Plum Clafouti 68
Brandy Orange Sauce 68
Bread Pudding, Fruity 50

Cake
    Austrian Coffee 58
    Berry Chocolate Mud 44
    Cassata alla Siciliana 36
    Coconut Angel Food 46
    Devil's Food 49
    French Christmas Log 38
    Orange and Almond Gâteau 60
    Triple-chocolate Terrine 12
Cakes
    Ginger Pear 34
    Raspberry Truffle 64

Caramel
    Banana Pie 24
    Sauce 18, 50
Cassata alla Siciliana 36
Cheesecake
    Lemon Sultana 48
    Orange and Lime 6
Cherry Pie 75
Chestnut Chocolate Truffles 76
Chocolate
    see also White Chocolate
    Berry Mud Cake 44
    Brownie Torte 28
    Butter Icing 49
    Chestnut Truffles 76
    Cream 33
    Cups 62
    Devil's Food Cake 49
    French Christmas Log 38
    Ganach Icing 38
    Jaffa Self-saucing Pudding 45
    Millefeuilles 33
    Mushrooms 38
    Orange Tarts 26
    Raspberry Truffle Cakes 64
    Sauce 64
    Terrine 12
Christmas Log, French 38
Christmas Pudding, Boiled 40
Clafouti, Brandied Plum 68
Cobbler, Peach and Berry 70
Coconut Angel Food Cake 46
Coeur à la Crème 52
Coffee
    Cake, Austrian 58
    Cream 58
    Ice Cream 14
    Nut Pie 24
Compote, Peach 54
Coulis
    Peach 15, 62
    Raspberry 44
Cream
    Chocolate 33
    Coeur à la 52
    Coffee 58
    Ginger 34
    Peach 62
    Raspberry 22, 64
    Ricotta 56
Creamy Caramel Banana Pie 24

Creamy Fruit Parfaits 34
Crème Brûlée, Blackberry 44
Crêpes, Hazelnut 72
Crumble
    Apple and Berry 70
    Nutty Plum 72
Custard-based Ice Cream 16
Dates with Orange Filling 30
Devil's Food Cake 49
Double Zabaglione Soufflé 10

Figs, Toffee with Sabayon 68
Filled Chocolate Cups 62
Flan, Raspberry Mousse 20
Florentines 78
Fool, Rhubarb 54
French Christmas Log 38
Fresh Berry Tart 62
Fritters, Banana 50
Fruit
    Layered Terrine 8
    Parfaits 34
    Poached 22
    Summer Wine Jelly 17
Fruity Bread Pudding 50

Gâteau, Orange and Almond 60
Ginger
    Cream 34
    Pear Cakes 34

Hazelnut
    Crêpes 72
    Pastry 55
    Pinwheels 11

Ice Cream
    Cassata alla Siciliana 36
    Chocolate 16
    Coffee 14
    Custard-based 16
    Mousse-based 14
    Peach 16
    Pink and White 10
    Raspberry 14
    Rocky Road 30

Individual Summer Puddings 57

Jaffa Self-saucing Pudding 45
Jelly, Summer Wine 17

Kiwifruit Sorbert 16

Layered-fruit Terrine 8
Lemon Sultana Cheesecake 48
Lime
    and Orange Cheesecake 6
    Sorbet 14
Lychees, Stuffed, with Sabayon 32

Mango
    and Passion Fruit Sorbet 16
    Soup with Sorbet 14
Marsala Sabayon 68
Millefeuilles, Chocolate 33
Miniature Profiteroles 78
Mousse, White Chocolate 15
Mousse-based Ice Cream 14

Nectarine Timbales 8
Nut, Coffee Pie 24
Nutty Plum Crumble 72

Orange
    and Almond Gâteau 60
    and Lime Cheesecake 6
    Biscuits 54
    Brandy Sauce 68
    Butter Cream 60
    Chocolate Tarts 26
    Cointreau Sauce 32
    Jaffa Self-saucing Pudding 45
    Sauce 8

Pancakes
    Berry, with Sauce 74
    with Orange Sauce 32
Parfaits, Creamy Fruit 34
Passion Fruit and Mango Sorbet 16
Pastry
    Almond 20
    Hazelnut 55
    Shortcrust 48
    Sweet Shortcrust 21
Pavlova 42
Peach
    and Berry Cobbler 70
    Compote 54
    Coulis 15, 62

Cream 62
Ice Cream 16
Pear Ginger Cakes 34
Pie
    Apple 75
    Apricot 74
    Cherry 75
    Coffee Nut 24
    Creamy Caramel Banana 24
    Sour Cream Apple 18
    Spicy Pumpkin 40
Pink and White Ice Cream 10
Pinwheels, Hazelnut 11
Plum
    Clafouti 68
    Crumble 72
Poached Fruit 22
Profiteroles, Miniature 78
Pudding
    Apple 56
    Apple and Berry Crumble 70
    Brandied Plum Clafouti 68
    Christmas, Boiled 40
    Fruity Bread 50
    Individual Summer 57
    Jaffa Self-saucing 45
    Nutty Plum Crumble 72
    Peach and Berry Cobbler 70
Pumpkin Pie, Spicy 40

Raspberry
    Coulis 44
    Cream 22, 64
    Ice Cream 14
    Mousse Flan 20
    Pink and White Ice Cream 10
    Tarts 55
    Truffle Cakes 64
Rhubarb
    and Apple Tart 26
    Fool 54
    Soufflé 66
Ricotta Cream 56
Rocky Road Ice Cream 30

Sabayon
    Berry 32
    Marsala 68

Sauce
    Berry 57, 74
    Brandy Orange 68
    Caramel 18, 50
    Chocolate 64
    Orange 8
    Orange Cointreau 32
Sorbet
    Kiwifruit 16
    Lime 14
    Mango and Passion Fruit 16
    Watermelon 16
Soufflé
    Double Zabaglione 10
    Rhubarb 66
Soup, Mango Coconut,
    with Sorbet 14
Sour Cream Apple Pie 18
Spicy Pumpkin Pie 40
Stuffed Lychees with Sabayon 32
Sugar-crusted Baskets 22
Summer Wine Jelly 17
Summer Puddings, Individual 57
Sweet Cinnamon Bows 77
Sweet Shortcrust Pastry 21

Tart
    Fresh Berry 62
    Orange Chocolate 26
    Raspberry 55
    Rhubarb and Apple 26
Terrine
    Layered-fruit 8
    Triple-chocolate 12
Timbales, Nectarine 8
Toffee Figs with Sabayon 68
Torte, Chocolate Brownie 28
Triple-chocolate Terrine 12
Truffles, Chocolate Chestnut 76

Watermelon Sorbet 16
White Chocolate
    Mousse 15
    Pink and White Ice Cream 10